the complete

COOKBOOK for TEEN CHEF

AMERICA'S TEST KITCHEN

OTHER COOKBOOKS BY AMERICA'S TEST KITCHEN KIDS

The Complete Cookbook for Young Chefs
#1 New York Times best seller, 2019 IACP Cookbook Award winner for Children, Youth & Family

The Complete Baby and Toddler Cookbook
2020 IACP Cookbook Award nominee for Children, Youth & Family

The Complete Baking Book for Young Chefs
New York Times best seller, 2020 IACP Cookbook Award winner for Children, Youth & Family

My First Cookbook

The Complete DIY Cookbook for Young Chefs
2021 IACP Cookbook Award nominee for Children, Youth & Family

The Complete Cookbook for Young Scientists

PRAISE FOR AMERICA'S TEST KITCHEN KIDS

"The inviting, encouraging tone, which never talks down to the audience; emphasis on introducing and reinforcing basic skills; and approachable, simplified recipes make this a notable standout among cookbooks for kids." —*Booklist*, starred review, on *The Complete Cookbook for Young Chefs*

"A must-have book . . . a great holiday buy, too."
—*School Library Journal*, on *The Complete Cookbook for Young Chefs*

"Inspiring not just a confidence in executing delicious recipes but encouraging them to build foundational kitchen skills." —The Takeout, on *The Complete Cookbook for Young Chefs*

"What a great way to encourage a child to find fun in the kitchen!"
—Tribune Content Agency, on *The Complete Cookbook for Young Chefs*

"For kids who are interested in cooking . . . [*The Complete Cookbook for Young Chefs*] introduces kids to all the basics . . . and of course there's a whole lot of easy and very tasty recipes to try." —NPR's *Morning Edition*, on *The Complete Cookbook for Young Chefs*

"Having cooked through several cookbooks from America's Test Kitchen, I have come to expect thoroughness, thoughtfulness, attention to detail and helpful troubleshooting, all of which create delicious results. It comes as no surprise that when ATK decided to create a cookbook for kids, *The Complete Cookbook for Young Chefs*, the same standards applied." —*Dallas Morning News*, on *The Complete Cookbook for Young Chefs*

"America's Test Kitchen has long been a reliable source of advice for home cooks. The kitchen tests tools, techniques and recipes before making recommendations through its TV show, magazines and cookbooks. Now, all that know-how is becoming accessible to kids in *The Complete Cookbook for Young Chefs*." —NPR, on *The Complete Cookbook for Young Chefs*

"This book makes baking accessible . . . An inclusive and welcoming text for young chefs." —*Booklist*, on *The Complete Baking Book for Young Chefs*

"A must-have book to keep your young adult cookbook section up-to-date and to support the current trend of creative young bakers. A contemporary and educational cookbook that's once again kid-tested and kid-approved." —*School Library Journal*, starred review, on *The Complete Baking Book for Young Chefs*

"The cooks at America's Test Kitchen have done a wonderful job of assembling appetizing and slyly audacious recipes for babies and young children." —*Wall Street Journal*, on *The Complete Baby and Toddler Cookbook*

"This wonderfully interactive, non-messy introduction to baking, though especially designed for preschoolers, will be an instant hit with readers of all ages." —*School Library Journal*, on *Stir Crack Whisk Bake*

"The story is a fun concept, and Tarkela's realistic digital illustration offers the pleasing details of a television studio." —*Publishers Weekly*, on *Cookies for Santa*

"This is the perfect subscription for the kid who loves food, picky eaters who you want to get into more adventurous foods, parents who want to share cooking fun with their kids, and generally, any kid who is up for a fun activity." —PopSugar, on the *Young Chefs' Club*

"Kids will love the colorful site and its plentiful selection of recipes, projects, and cooking lessons." —*USA Today*, on America's Test Kitchen Kids website

Library of Congress Cataloging-in-Publication Data
Names: America's Test Kitchen (Firm)
Title: The complete cookbook for teen chefs : 70+ teen-tested and teen-approved recipes to cook, eat, and share / America's Test Kitchen.
Description: Boston, MA : America's Test Kitchen, [2022] | Includes index. | Audience: Ages 14 to 18 | Audience: Grades 10-12
Identifiers: LCCN 2021052775 (print) | LCCN 2021052776 (ebook) | ISBN 9781948703956 (hardcover) | ISBN 9781948703963 (ebook)
Subjects: LCSH: Cooking--Juvenile literature. | Quick and easy cooking--Juvenile literature. | LCGFT: Cookbooks.
Classification: LCC TX652.5 .C6323 2022 (print) | LCC TX652.5 (ebook) | DDC 641.5--dc23/ eng/20211028
LC record available at https://lccn.loc.gov/2021052775
LC ebook record available at https://lccn.loc.gov/2021052776

AMERICA'S TEST KITCHEN
21 Drydock Avenue, Boston, MA 02210

Printed in Canada
9 8 7 6 5 4 3 2 1

Distributed by Penguin Random House Publisher Services
Tel: 800.733.3000

FRONT COVER
Photography: Kevin White

Food Styling: Ashley Moore

Editor in Chief: Molly Birnbaum

Executive Food Editor: Suzannah McFerran

Executive Editor: Kristin Sargianis

Senior Editors: Ali Velez Alderfer, Afton Cyrus

Test Cooks: Cassandra Loftlin, Andrea Rivera Wawrzyn

Assistant Test Cook: Kristen Bango

Associate Editors: Tess Berger, Katy O'Hara

Editorial Assistant: Julia Arwine

Design Director: Lindsey Timko Chandler

Graphic Designer, Books: Molly Gillespie

Associate Art Director: Gabi Homonoff

Photography Director: Julie Bozzo Cote

Photographers: Kevin White, Joe Keller, Steve Klise

Food Styling: Joy Howard, Chantal Lambeth, Ashley Moore, Christie Morrison, Kendra Smith

Photography Producer: Meredith Mulcahy

Photo Shoot Kitchen Team

> **Test Kitchen Director:** Erin McMurrer
>
> **Photo Team Manager:** Alli Berkey
>
> **Lead Test Cook:** Eric Haessler
>
> **Test Cooks:** Hannah Fenton, Jacqueline Gochenouer, Gina McCreadie
>
> **Assistant Test Cooks:** Hisham Hassan, Christa West

Senior Manager, Publishing Operations: Taylor Argenzio

Senior Print Production Specialist: Lauren Robbins

Production and Imaging Specialists: Tricia Neumyer, Dennis Noble, Amanda Yong

Lead Copy Editor: Rachel Schowalter

Copy Editors: Christine Campbell, April Poole

Chief Creative Officer: Jack Bishop

Executive Editorial Directors: Julia Collin Davison, Bridget Lancaster

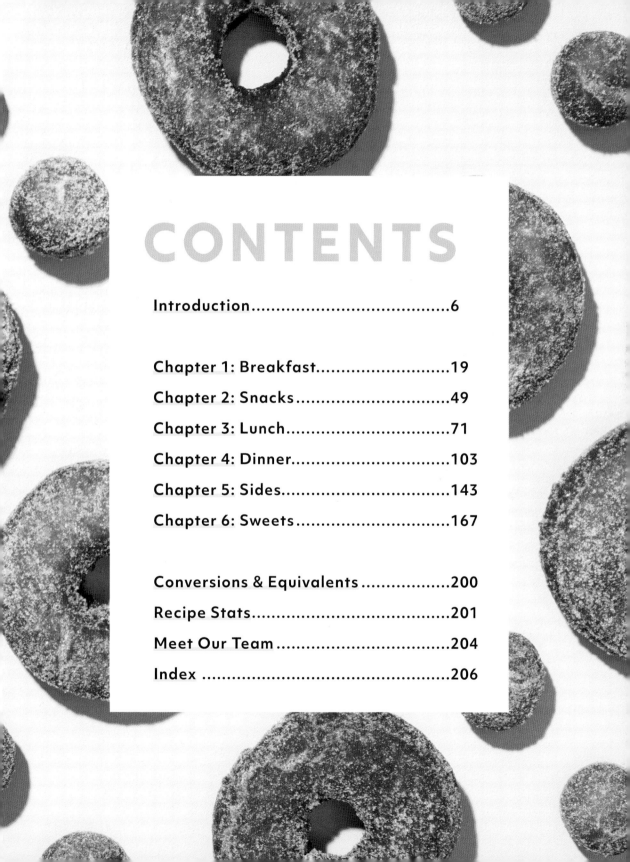

CONTENTS

Welcome to America's Test Kitchen!

We are a team of cooks, writers, editors, designers, and photographers working in a professional test kitchen in Boston (see more about us on page 204). We're serious about food! And we're serious about fun, too. We created this book to inspire you to get in the kitchen, feel confident as you cook, and have fun making great food with your friends and family.

This book is teen tested and teen approved. This means that thousands of teens tested each and every recipe in this book at home and sent us feedback about what worked well and what could use improvement. In fact, we only publish a recipe if at least 80 percent of our teen testers said that they would make the recipe again. You'll see quotes from many of these recipe testers throughout the book. Thank you to everyone who helped make this book as delicious as possible!

Cooking and baking are science as well as art. Whether you're just starting out or have been cooking for years, don't be surprised if you have questions or make mistakes (we still do, ourselves). The important thing is to just cook! Don't be afraid to experiment. Mistakes are still often pretty delicious (and they make good stories, too).

HOW TO USE THIS BOOK

As you flip through this book and decide what to cook, be sure to take a look at the tags in the top-left corner of each recipe page. Each recipe is assigned a skill level of beginner, intermediate, or advanced, and vegetarian recipes are noted, too.

Once you're ready to get started, keep in mind that organization is key to success in the kitchen and that the recipes in this book are written to help keep you on track. If you prepare your ingredients ahead of time, you won't wind up frantically chopping herbs or measuring out flour at the last minute. Before you get started, scan the recipe to find all the highlighted equipment—that's what you'll need to have on hand to cook through the recipe.

PREPARE INGREDIENTS

Start with the list of ingredients and prepare them as directed. Wash fruits and vegetables, measure ingredients, melt butter, chop, mince, and so on. You can use small prep bowls to keep the ingredients organized.

START COOKING!

Any ingredients that need to be prepped at the last minute will have instructions within the recipe steps. Make sure that you note the highlighted equipment throughout the recipe and have it ready.

3 SECRETS TO SUCCESS

(IN THE KITCHEN)

Cooking isn't rocket science, but it does require attention to detail. Here are three secrets to becoming a kitchen pro.

▶ SECRET #1: READ CAREFULLY

Whether you're new in the kitchen or an experienced cook, always start by reading the entire recipe. Check out the key stats: How much food does the recipe make? How long will it take? Then make sure that you have the right ingredients and equipment on hand. The first time you make a recipe, follow the steps as written. You can always improvise once you understand how the recipe works. (And if there are phrases in the recipe that you're not familiar with, see "Key Recipe Terms," page 15.)

▶ SECRET #2: STAY FOCUSED

Just like playing a sport, making a piece of art, or coding an app, cooking requires focus. Incorrect measurements can lead to overseasoned food (too much salt) or flat cakes (too little baking powder). Pay attention to both the visual cues ("cook until well browned") and the times ("cook for 5 minutes") in the recipe. If the recipe has a time range, set your timer to the lower number. You can always keep cooking if necessary, but there's no going back once food is overcooked.

▶ SECRET #3: MISTAKES ARE OK

First things first: Don't sweat it. Try to figure out what you would do differently next time. Maybe you should have set a timer so that you would remember to check your eggs before they overcook, or maybe you should have double-checked that you actually had enough flour before you started the recipe. And if your food isn't perfect, don't worry—a misshapen cookie is still delicious.

KITCHEN SAFETY

Just about every recipe involves a small element of danger, from sharp knives to a hot stovetop. Follow the steps and tips on these pages to help you stay safe in the kitchen.

HOW TO USE KNIVES SAFELY

The two knives you'll use most frequently are a small paring knife, for precision work such as coring tomatoes, and a larger chef's knife, for everything from mincing herbs to cutting vegetables to slicing meat. Here are two important things to remember when using knives.

Protect Your Fingertips: While you're **chopping**, always use a "bear claw" grip to hold food in place and minimize danger—tuck your fingertips in, keeping them away from the knife. During the upward part of the slicing motion, reposition your "clawed" hand for the next cut. While you're **mincing**, rest the fingers of the hand not gripping the knife on top of the blade, away from the tip.

Sharp Knives Are Safe Knives: A dull knife is an accident waiting to happen. That's because it's much more likely to slip off food while you're using it. To tell if your knife is sharp, hold up a sheet of basic printer paper by one end. Lay the knife blade against the top edge at an angle, and then slice outward (away from you). If the knife slices cleanly, it's sharp! If it drags, it needs sharpening. If you need to sharpen your knife, you can use either electric or manual sharpeners.

HOW TO TELL WHEN MEAT OR FISH IS DONE

The most reliable way to know when thick cuts of chicken, meat, or fish are cooked is to use an instant-read thermometer.

To check the temperature, insert the tip of the instant-read thermometer into the center of the thickest part of the food, making sure to avoid any bones. You can use tongs to lift individual pieces of chicken, meat, or fish and then insert the thermometer sideways into the food.

Key Temperatures: Recipes often give a specific temperature for cooking different proteins, which tells you when the food is hot enough to eat.

Beef

115 to 120 degrees (rare)
120 to 125 degrees (medium-rare)
130 to 135 degrees (medium)
140 to 145 degrees (medium–well done)
150 to 155 degrees (well-done)

Chicken

160 degrees (white meat)
175 degrees (dark meat)

Salmon

120 degrees for wild-caught
125 degrees for farm-raised

HOW TO SAFELY HANDLE RAW MEAT, FISH, AND EGGS

After handling raw meat, fish, or eggs, always wash your hands, cutting boards, and counters (and anything else that came into contact with the raw ingredients, their juices, or your hands) with hot, soapy water. Be especially careful not to let raw meat, fish, or eggs; their juices; or your unwashed hands touch foods that will be eaten raw (such as salad greens). Also, the United States Department of Agriculture (USDA) advises against rinsing raw poultry. Doing so will not remove much bacteria, and any splashing water can spread bacteria found on the surface of the raw chicken.

HOW TO FRY SAFELY

You can make restaurant-quality fried food at home—if you're careful. Follow these tips to help you fry successfully (and safely).

▶ Use a Large Pot

Using a large Dutch oven (one that holds 6 to 7 quarts) ensures that the oil won't rise too high after you add the food you're frying.

▶ An Instant-Read Thermometer Is Your Best Friend

Always follow the temperature cues in the recipe. If the oil starts lightly smoking, that's a sign that it's overheated—turn off the heat until the oil cools to the correct temperature.

▶ Use the Right Tool

Use a slotted spoon or spider skimmer to remove smaller foods, such as french fries, from the frying oil—any excess oil will drain through their holes.

▶ When You're Done Frying

Once you're finished frying, turn off the heat, cover the pot with a lid, and allow the oil to cool completely. Never pour frying oil down the drain! Once the oil is cool, you can use a large liquid measuring cup and funnel to pour it into its original container and then throw it away. You can also reuse frying oil three to four times if it's been used to fry chicken and up to eight times if it was used for french fries.

To reuse your oil, set a fine-mesh strainer in a large liquid measuring cup and line it with a coffee filter. Carefully pour the oil through the strainer, and then discard any solids. Pour the oil into its original container and store it until you're ready to use it again.

ESSENTIAL HOW-TOS

How to Measure Ice Water

Fill large glass with ice and water and place glass in refrigerator until you need it. Place liquid measuring cup on scale (if using) and tare scale. Hold fine-mesh strainer above measuring cup. Pour water through fine-mesh strainer to measure desired amount of water. Discard ice.

HOW TO MEASURE AND WEIGH

For consistent cooking results, it's important to measure accurately. There are two ways to measure ingredients: by weight (using a scale) and by volume (using measuring cups and spoons). Using a scale to weigh your ingredients is the most accurate. But if you don't have a scale, that's OK! Below are tips both for how to use a scale and how best to measure ingredients if you don't have one.

How to Measure Dry and Liquid Ingredients

Note that small amounts of both dry and liquid ingredients are measured with measuring spoons.

How to Use a Scale

Dry ingredients should be measured in dry measuring cups. Dip measuring cup into ingredient and sweep away excess with back of butter knife.

Liquid ingredients should be measured in a liquid measuring cup. Set measuring cup on counter and bend down to read bottom of concave arc at liquid's surface. (This is known as the meniscus line.)

1. Turn on scale and place bowl on scale. Press "tare" button to zero out weight (that means that the weight of the bowl won't be included).

2. Slowly add ingredient to bowl until you reach desired weight. (Here, we are weighing 5 ounces of all-purpose flour, which is equal to 1 cup.)

HOW TO CHOP AND MINCE

Depending on the recipe, you might be asked to chop or mince ingredients. Recipes might tell you to chop fine (making ⅛- to ¼-inch pieces), chop (making ¼- to ½-inch pieces), or chop coarse (making ½- to ¾-inch pieces). Mincing makes even smaller pieces, ⅛ inch or smaller. As you chop something large, such as a bell pepper, you'll usually first slice the food into strips. Then you'll cut the strips crosswise (the short way) into pieces.

How to Chop Onions or Shallots: Shallots are smaller, milder cousins to onions. If you're working with a small shallot, there's no need to cut it in half.

1. Place onion on cutting board and use chef's knife to cut onion in half through root end, then use your fingers to remove peel.

2. Place onion half flat side down. Trim top of onion and discard. Starting 1 inch from root end, make several vertical cuts.

3. Rotate onion and slice across first cuts. As you slice, onion will fall apart into chopped pieces.

How to Slice Onions

Place onion on cutting board and use chef's knife to cut onion in half through root end, then use your fingers to remove peel. Place onion halves flat side down. Trim off ends and discard. Slice onion vertically into thin strips, following grain (long stripes on onion).

How to Mince Garlic and Herbs

Place garlic or herbs on cutting board in small pile. Place your hand on handle of chef's knife and rest fingers of your other hand on top of blade. Use rocking motion, pivoting knife as you chop food repeatedly to cut it into very small pieces.

HOW TO PREP AN AVOCADO

Here's an easy way to open and remove the pit of a ripe avocado.

1. Place avocado on cutting board. Use chef's knife to cut avocado in half lengthwise (the long way) around pit.

2. Using your hands, twist both halves in opposite directions to separate.

3. Use spoon to scoop out pit; discard pit.

4. Use spoon to scoop out avocado from skin; discard skin. Avocado can now be sliced, chopped, or mashed.

HOW TO PREP CHILES

Chiles contain a compound called capsaicin that makes them spicy. To make sure that you do not get it on your skin or in your eyes, make sure to wear disposable gloves when touching chiles.

1. Place chile on cutting board. Hold chile firmly with your hand, with stem facing out. Use chef's knife to slice off stem and top of chile.

2. Cut chile in half lengthwise (the long way). Use tip of teaspoon to scoop out seeds and ribs from each half. Discard seeds, ribs, and stem.

3. Press 1 half of chile so it lays flat, skin side down. Slice chile lengthwise (the long way) into ¼-inch-wide strips. Repeat with remaining chile half.

4. Turn strips and cut crosswise (the short way) into ¼-inch pieces. Repeat with remaining chile half.

▶ SEASON TO TASTE

Some recipes tell you to "season to taste" just before serving. That usually means adding a bit more salt (and sometimes pepper or an acidic ingredient, such as lime juice). Here's how to do it: Taste your finished recipe. Is it a little bland? Could it use more flavor? If so, it probably needs a bit of salt. Add a pinch of salt, stir (if necessary), and taste again. Repeat adding a pinch of salt and tasting until you're happy with the flavor of your dish. But remember: A tiny bit of salt can have a big impact on flavor, so go slow—you can always add more salt.

▶ HEATING OIL

When you heat oil in a pan, there are two visual cues that a recipe will tell you to look for: shimmering and just smoking. When oil is **shimmering**, it moves slightly and looks like it has little waves across its surface. When oil just begins to **smoke**, you'll start to see wisps of smoke coming up from the oil. This is easier to see if you bend down and get eye level with the pan.

▶ DON'T OVERMIX

To keep muffins, pancakes, and quick breads as light and tender as possible, the key is to not overmix the batter. This means mixing until all the ingredients are just combined, usually until there is no more dry flour visible (there might be some lumps in your batter—this is OK). Why? The more you mix, the more the proteins in the flour combine to form gluten. And the more gluten, the tougher the final product.

▶ SWITCHING AND ROTATING BAKING SHEETS

Sometimes, a recipe asks you to rotate the baking sheet halfway through baking—that means to turn the pan 180 degrees on the oven rack. This is important because most ovens don't heat evenly—rotating the pan helps promote even cooking on whatever is in the oven. If you have two baking sheets in the oven at the same time, you need to rotate the baking sheets 180 degrees AND flip-flop which racks they're on.

KEY RECIPE TERMS

ESSENTIAL KITCHEN GEAR

Here is the equipment you'll use over and over in the kitchen, from small appliances to prep tools to knives and more.

SMALL APPLIANCES

▼ Stand mixer

◀ Blender

▲ Immersion blender

▲ Food processor

▲ Electric handheld mixer

KNIVES

▲ Chef's knife

▶ Cutting board

▲ Paring knife

COOKWARE AND BAKEWARE

Skillet, traditional metal (12-inch) ▼

Skillets, nonstick ▼
(12-inch and 10-inch)

9-inch round metal cake pan

▲ 8½-by-4½-inch metal loaf pan

▲ Large saucepan
(3- to 4-quart)

Cooling rack

▲ Dutch oven
(6- to 7-quart)

▲ 10-inch cast-iron skillet

▲ 8-inch and 13-by-9-inch metal baking pans

▲ 12-cup muffin tin

Rimmed baking sheet

KITCHEN BASICS

▶ Prep bowls

▶ Dish towels

◀ Oven mitts

PREP TOOLS

Scale ▶

◀ Box grater

◀ Ruler

◀ Rasp grater

Dry measuring cups ▶

◀ Garlic press

Citrus juicer ▶

◀ Liquid measuring cup

Can opener ▶

◀ Measuring spoons

Vegetable peeler ▶

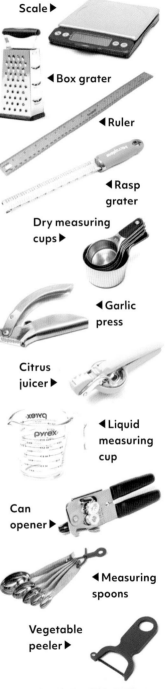

COOKING AND BAKING TOOLS

▲ Rubber spatula

◀ Instant-read thermometer

Wooden spoon ▼

▲ Whisk

Tongs ▼

Ladle ▼

Spatula ▼

Potato masher ▶

Fine-mesh strainer ▼

◀ Pastry brush

◀ Colander

Bench scraper ▶

Icing spatula (offset) ▶

▲ Rolling pin

chapter 1
BREAKFAST

BREAKFAST SANDWICHES

BEFORE YOU BEGIN

▶ Make sure to cook your bacon or sausage patties before you start this recipe.

PREPARE INGREDIENTS

4   slices cooked bacon (see page 75)
    or 2 cooked sausage patties

2   large eggs

1   pinch plus 1 pinch salt,
    measured separately

1   pinch plus 1 pinch pepper,
    measured separately

1   tablespoon unsalted butter, melted

2   rolls or English muffins (page 44),
    cut or split in half

1   teaspoon vegetable oil

2   slices American or cheddar cheese

FOR PERFECTLY FRIED EGGS, PUT A LID ON IT

The ideal fried egg—with a cooked white and a runny yolk—can be tricky to make because egg whites and egg yolks set at different temperatures. Egg whites are fully cooked at 180 degrees, while egg yolks begin to thicken at 150 degrees and are fully set at 158 degrees.

One way to get fully set whites without overcooking the yolks? Steam. In this recipe, we cover the skillet with a lid while the eggs cook—this traps steam and heats the eggs from the top and the bottom.

START COOKING!

1. Crack large eggs into 2 small bowls (1 egg per bowl). Add 1 pinch salt and 1 pinch pepper to each bowl.

2. Use pastry brush to spread melted butter evenly over cut sides of rolls. Add rolls, buttered side down, to 10-inch nonstick skillet.

3. Cook rolls over medium heat until cut sides are golden brown, 3 to 5 minutes. Use spatula to transfer rolls, cut sides up, to serving plates.

4. Add oil to now-empty skillet. Increase heat to medium-high and heat oil for 30 seconds (oil should be hot but not smoking).

5. Working quickly, pour eggs into opposite sides of skillet. Cover skillet with lid and cook for 1 minute. Turn off heat and slide skillet to cool burner. Carefully flip eggs.

6. Place 1 slice cheese on top of each egg. Cover skillet and let sit for about 1 minute for slightly runny yolks or about 2 minutes for set yolks.

7. Add 2 slices cooked bacon or 1 cooked sausage patty to each roll bottom. Place 1 cooked egg on top of bacon or sausage. Cap sandwiches with roll tops. Serve immediately.

SHAKSHUKA

(Eggs in Spicy Tomato and Red Pepper Sauce)

BEFORE YOU BEGIN

▶ If you have a glass lid for your skillet, this is a great place to use it—you'll be able to see the eggs as they're cooking.

PREPARE INGREDIENTS

- 2 (8-inch) pitas
- 1 (12-ounce) jar roasted red peppers, drained
- 1 (14.5-ounce) can whole peeled tomatoes, drained
- 2 garlic cloves, peeled and sliced thin
- 1½ teaspoons tomato paste
- 1 teaspoon ground coriander
- 1 teaspoon smoked paprika
- ½ teaspoon ground cumin
- ¼ teaspoon salt
- ⅛ teaspoon pepper
- ⅛ teaspoon cayenne pepper
- 2 tablespoons extra-virgin olive oil
- 4 large eggs
- ¼ cup chopped fresh cilantro (see page 13)
- 2 tablespoons crumbled feta cheese

START COOKING!

1. Place pitas on cutting board. Use chef's knife to cut each pita into 8 wedges. Then, cut 1 wedge into ½-inch pieces and add to blender jar. Save remaining pita wedges for serving.

2. Add half of drained red peppers to blender jar. Transfer remaining drained red peppers to cutting board. Chop into ¼-inch pieces; set aside.

3. Add drained tomatoes to blender jar. Place lid on top of blender and hold lid firmly in place with folded dish towel. Process mixture until smooth, about 1 minute.

4. In small bowl, combine garlic, tomato paste, coriander, paprika, cumin, salt, pepper, and cayenne.

5. In 10-inch skillet, heat oil over medium heat until shimmering, about 2 minutes (oil should be hot but not smoking). Add garlic mixture and cook, stirring often with rubber spatula, until fragrant, about 30 seconds. Turn off heat and slide skillet to cool burner.

keep going >>>

SHAKSHUKA: A ONE-PAN WONDER

Savory shakshuka originally hails from North Africa but arrived with Jewish immigrants to the Middle East, where it remains popular—particularly in Israel. Cooking the eggs directly in the spiced tomato sauce—and spooning some of the sauce over the egg whites—helps them cook evenly, from the outside in. The bottoms, sides, and tops of the whites (which are on the outside of the egg) are in contact with the simmering sauce and the hot steam trapped under the skillet's lid, meaning that they start to cook first. It takes a little longer for the heat to reach the yolks, so they cook more slowly. The results? Fully cooked egg whites surrounding perfectly runny yolks. Brunch is served.

6. Carefully pour blended tomato mixture into skillet (mixture may splatter). Add chopped red peppers and stir to combine. Return skillet to medium heat and bring to simmer (small bubbles should break often across surface of mixture).

7. Reduce heat to medium-low and cook, stirring occasionally, until thickened (spatula will leave trail that slowly fills in behind it, but sauce will still slosh when skillet is shaken), about 15 minutes.

8. Turn off heat and slide skillet to cool burner. Assemble shakshuka following photos, right.

9. Return skillet to medium heat and cook until mixture is bubbling all over, about 1 minute. Reduce heat to medium-low. Cover skillet with lid and cook until yolks film over, 3 to 4 minutes.

10. Continue to cook, covered, until whites are softly set (if skillet is shaken lightly, each egg should jiggle as a single unit), 1 to 2 minutes.

11. Turn off heat and slide skillet to cool burner. Sprinkle with cilantro and feta. Season with salt and pepper to taste (see page 15). Serve immediately with pita wedges.

"It would be good for breakfast or dinner!"
—Georgia, 16

HOW TO ASSEMBLE SHAKSHUKA

1. Use back of spoon to make shallow hole (about the size of a quarter) in sauce.

2. Crack 1 egg into clean small bowl. Carefully pour egg into hole (it will hold yolk in place but not fully contain whites). Repeat with remaining 3 eggs, making 3 more holes, spaced evenly apart.

3. Spoon sauce over edges of egg whites so whites are partially covered and yolks are exposed.

SHEET-PAN HASH BROWNS

BEFORE YOU BEGIN

▶ If you don't have a food processor with a shredding disk, you can grate the potatoes by hand on the large holes of a box grater.

PREPARE INGREDIENTS

Vegetable oil spray

2 pounds Yukon Gold potatoes, unpeeled

¼ cup extra-virgin olive oil

¾ teaspoon salt

¼ teaspoon pepper

FOR THE BEST HASH BROWNS, GET RID OF THE WATER

Moisture is the enemy of browning, and potatoes are made up of mostly water and starch (which absorbs water when heated). So to maximize the brown and crispy bits in our hash browns, we use two tricks. First, we give the shredded potatoes a quick soak to remove excess water-absorbing starch on their surface. And then we squeeze, squeeze, squeeze.

HOW TO SQUEEZE POTATOES DRY

Place one-quarter of shredded potatoes in center of clean dish towel. Gather ends of towel together, twist tightly, and squeeze over sink to drain as much liquid as possible from potatoes. Transfer dried potatoes to now-empty bowl. Repeat 3 more times with remaining potatoes.

START COOKING!

1. Adjust oven rack to middle position and heat oven to 450 degrees. Lightly spray rimmed baking sheet with vegetable oil spray. Set colander in sink.

2. Place potatoes on cutting board. Use chef's knife to cut potatoes into halves or quarters so they fit in food processor feed tube. Fit food processor with shredding disk. Place a few potato pieces in feed tube. With processor running, push potatoes down with plunger to shred. Repeat with remaining potatoes. Remove lid and carefully remove disk.

3. Transfer potatoes to large bowl. Cover with cold water. Let sit for 5 minutes.

4. One handful at a time, lift potatoes out of water and transfer to colander in sink; discard water. Rinse and dry bowl.

5. Working in 4 batches, squeeze potatoes dry in dish towel and transfer to now-empty bowl, following photo, below left.

6. Add oil, salt, and pepper to potatoes and use your hands to mix until well combined.

7. Spread potatoes in even layer on greased baking sheet, making sure to spread to edges. Do not pack down potatoes.

8. Bake potatoes until top is spotty brown, 30 to 35 minutes.

9. Use oven mitts to transfer baking sheet to cooling rack. Use spatula to break up hash browns into large pieces and flip hash browns. Continue to bake until light golden brown on top, 5 to 10 minutes. Transfer baking sheet to cooling rack. Serve.

GERMAN PANCAKE

BEFORE YOU BEGIN

▶ A traditional 12-inch skillet can be used instead of the nonstick; coat it well with vegetable oil spray before adding butter in step 3.

▶ As an alternative to sprinkling sugar and lemon juice over your pancake, try it with maple syrup or our Brown Sugar–Banana Topping (see right).

PREPARE INGREDIENTS

1¾ cups (8¾ ounces) all-purpose flour

1 tablespoon grated lemon zest plus 1 tablespoon juice (zested and squeezed from 1 lemon)

½ teaspoon salt

⅛ teaspoon ground nutmeg

3 tablespoons plus 1 tablespoon sugar, measured separately

1½ cups (12 ounces) milk

6 large eggs

1½ teaspoons vanilla extract

3 tablespoons unsalted butter, cut into 3 pieces

BROWN SUGAR– BANANA TOPPING

2 tablespoons unsalted butter

¼ cup packed (1¾ ounces) brown sugar

2 tablespoons water

1 teaspoon lemon juice (squeezed from ½ lemon)

¼ teaspoon ground cardamom

⅛ teaspoon salt

3 ripe bananas, peeled and sliced crosswise on bias into ⅛-inch-thick pieces

In 10-inch skillet, melt butter over medium heat. Add brown sugar, water, lemon juice, cardamom, and salt and whisk until well combined. Add bananas and cook, stirring often with rubber spatula, until mixture thickens and bananas are soft around edges, 2 to 3 minutes. Turn off heat. Transfer bananas to bowl and serve warm.

START COOKING!

1. In large bowl, whisk together flour, lemon zest, salt, nutmeg, and 3 tablespoons sugar. In medium bowl, whisk milk, eggs, and vanilla until smooth.

2. Add two-thirds of milk mixture to flour mixture and whisk until there are no lumps. Add remaining milk mixture and whisk gently until combined.

3. Adjust oven rack to lower-middle position. In 12-inch ovensafe nonstick skillet, melt butter over medium-low heat. When butter is completely melted, add batter to skillet and turn off heat.

4. Immediately place skillet in cold oven. Heat oven to 375 degrees. Bake until pancake is puffed, edges are deep golden brown, and center is beginning to brown, 30 to 35 minutes. (This is a good time to make the Brown Sugar–Banana Topping [see below left], if making.)

5. Use oven mitts to transfer skillet to cooling rack. Place oven mitt on skillet handle as a reminder that handle is HOT. Sprinkle pancake with lemon juice and remaining 1 tablespoon sugar.

6. Use spatula to gently slide pancake onto cutting board. (Pancake will deflate a little bit, but that is OK!) Use chef's knife to cut pancake into wedges. Serve.

THE ORIGINAL DUTCH BABY

The original German pfannkuchen (literally "pan cake") first appeared on the menu as a "Dutch baby" at Manca's Cafe in Seattle in the early 1900s. And not because they were inspired by the Netherlands: When the café owner's daughter first saw one of these big German pancakes, she mispronounced the word "Deutsch" ("German") as "Dutch." They added on the "baby" because the café's version, unlike ours, was small.

BEGINNER

SERVES 2 TO 4 / 30 MINUTES
(makes 7 round or
4 large square waffles)
plus time to cook bacon

BUTTERMILK WAFFLES

*with Bacon,
Cheddar,
and Scallions*

BEFORE YOU BEGIN

▶ The cornmeal adds extra crackle and crunch to the exterior of the waffles, but you can skip it if you don't have any on hand.

▶ Serve with maple syrup for a sweet-salty combo, hot sauce or chili crisp for a kick of heat, a drizzle of crema, or a fried egg on top.

"I really loved the combination of flavors; although unexpected, they complement each other perfectly!"
—Maxima, 16

PREPARE INGREDIENTS

4 slices cooked bacon (see page 75), crumbled

2 cups (10 ounces) all-purpose flour

2 tablespoons cornmeal (optional)

2 teaspoons baking soda

½ teaspoon salt

1¾ cups (14 ounces) buttermilk

2 large eggs

4 tablespoons unsalted butter, melted

1 cup shredded sharp cheddar cheese (4 ounces)

2 scallions, root ends trimmed and scallions chopped fine

Vegetable oil spray

▶ ▶ ▶ *UP YOUR GAME*

Mix and match different ingredients to make these waffles just the way you like them. In place of bacon, cheddar cheese, and scallions, try:

Meats: ¼ cup crumbled cooked **breakfast** or **lap cheong sausage**; finely chopped cured **Spanish-style chorizo** or **deli ham**

Vegetables and Herbs: 2 tablespoons finely chopped **onion**; 2 teaspoons minced **fresh thyme**, **rosemary**, or **parsley**

Cheeses: 1 cup shredded **Monterey Jack**, **pepper Jack**, **Colby**, or **Gruyère**; ½ cup finely grated **Parmesan cheese**

Other Flavors: 1 seeded and minced fresh **chile** (see page 14); 1 cup drained and chopped **cabbage kimchi**; 1 teaspoon **chili oil**

START COOKING!

1. Place cooling rack in rimmed baking sheet. Adjust oven rack to middle position and place baking sheet in oven. Heat oven to 200 degrees. Heat waffle iron.

2. In large bowl, whisk together flour, cornmeal (if using), baking soda, and salt. In medium bowl, whisk together buttermilk, eggs, and melted butter.

3. Add buttermilk mixture to flour mixture and use rubber spatula to stir until just combined and no dry flour remains. Add cheddar, scallions, and crumbled bacon and stir gently until just combined.

4. When waffle iron is hot, spray lightly with vegetable oil spray. Use dry measuring cups and rubber spatula to scoop batter and scrape into middle of waffle iron (use about ¾ cup batter for 7-inch round waffle iron or about 1½ cups batter for 9-inch square waffle iron). Spread batter into even layer. Close waffle iron and cook until waffle is golden brown.

5. Use fork to transfer waffle to baking sheet in oven to keep warm. Repeat with remaining batter. Serve.

AWESOME ACID

Buttermilk, a slightly sour ingredient, gives these savory waffles their light, fluffy interiors. Acidic buttermilk reacts with baking soda to produce carbon dioxide gas, creating bubbles in the batter. When the batter solidifies in the hot waffle iron, some of the bubbles are trapped inside, creating these waffles' airy texture. Traditionally, buttermilk is made from the liquid left over after churning cream into butter, but today most of the buttermilk you find at the grocery store is cultured buttermilk, made from milk that's been fermented using bacteria.

WHOLE-WHEAT BLUEBERRY MUFFINS

with Streusel Topping

BEFORE YOU BEGIN

▶ You can substitute frozen blueberries for fresh in this recipe; do not thaw them before using.

"The muffin looks and smells just as good as it tastes."
—Skyler, 15

PREPARE INGREDIENTS

STREUSEL

- 3 tablespoons packed brown sugar
- 3 tablespoons granulated sugar
- 3 tablespoons whole-wheat flour
- Pinch salt
- 2 tablespoons unsalted butter, melted

MUFFINS

- Vegetable oil spray
- 2½ teaspoons baking powder
- ½ teaspoon baking soda
- 3 cups (16½ ounces) whole-wheat flour
- 1 teaspoon salt
- 2 large eggs
- ¼ cup vegetable oil
- 1 cup (7 ounces) granulated sugar
- 4 tablespoons unsalted butter, melted and cooled
- 1¼ cups (10 ounces) buttermilk
- 1½ teaspoons vanilla extract
- 1½ cups (7½ ounces) blueberries

TENDER MUFFINS

One-hundred-percent whole-wheat muffins can be dense and squat. To make our version lighter and more tender, we combined two leaveners (baking powder and baking soda) for extra lift and added ingredients with a lot of water (buttermilk, eggs, blueberries, and butter) to keep these muffins moist, not dry.

START COOKING!

1. For the streusel: In small bowl, combine brown sugar, 3 tablespoons granulated sugar, 3 tablespoons flour, and pinch salt. Add 2 tablespoons melted butter and toss with fork until mixture is evenly moistened and forms large chunks with some pea-size pieces throughout; set aside.

2. For the muffins: Adjust oven rack to middle position and heat oven to 400 degrees. Spray 12-cup muffin tin, including top, well with vegetable oil spray.

3. In medium bowl, whisk together baking powder, baking soda, 3 cups flour, and 1 teaspoon salt.

4. In large bowl, whisk eggs, oil, 1 cup granulated sugar, and 4 tablespoons melted butter until combined, about 30 seconds. Add buttermilk and vanilla to egg mixture and whisk until combined.

5. Add flour mixture to egg mixture. Use rubber spatula to stir gently until just combined and no dry flour is visible. Gently stir blueberries into batter. Do not overmix (see page 15).

6. Spray ⅓-cup dry measuring cup with vegetable oil spray. Use greased measuring cup to divide batter evenly among greased muffin cups. Sprinkle streusel evenly over batter.

7. Bake until muffins are golden brown and toothpick inserted in center of 1 muffin comes out with few crumbs attached, 18 to 20 minutes, using oven mitts to rotate muffin tin halfway through baking (see page 15).

8. Transfer muffin tin to cooling rack. Let muffins cool in muffin tin for 5 minutes. Remove muffins from muffin tin and transfer directly to cooling rack. Let cool 5 minutes longer before serving.

HEARTY AVOCADO TOAST

BEFORE YOU BEGIN

▶ To tell if an avocado is ripe, gently squeeze it in the palm of your hand—if it's a little soft, it's ripe.

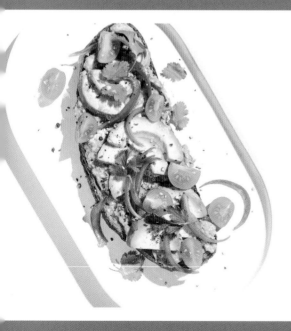

PREPARE INGREDIENTS

1 ripe avocado, halved and pitted
(see page 14)

2 teaspoons extra-virgin olive oil

2 teaspoons lemon juice, squeezed
from ½ lemon

⅛ teaspoon salt

Pinch pepper

2 (½-inch-thick) slices crusty bread

Toppings (see Up Your Game, below)

▶ ▶ ▶ **UP YOUR GAME**
Add even more flavor, texture, and color
to your avocado toast with toppings such
as **Pickled Red Onions** (see page 97),
crumbled **cooked bacon** (see page 75),
quartered **cherry tomatoes**, mashed
beans, fresh **herbs**, **chili crisp**, or even a
fried egg. Or try sprinkling it with your
favorite spice blend.

START COOKING!

1. Use spoon to scoop avocado halves onto
cutting board. Use chef's knife to cut 1 half of
avocado into ½-inch pieces. Cut second half into
thin slices.

2. In small bowl, whisk together oil, lemon juice,
salt, and pepper. Add chopped avocado to bowl
and use whisk to mash until mostly smooth and
well combined with dressing.

3. Toast bread until golden on both sides,
1 to 2 minutes. Spread mashed avocado evenly
over each piece of toast.

4. Arrange avocado slices evenly over top. Add
your favorite toppings. Season with salt and
pepper to taste (see page 15). Serve.

THIS TOAST IS ALL ABOUT TEXTURE AND TOPPINGS

Crunchy bread, creamy avocado, and the
bright punch of a simple lemon dressing
create the foundation of this toast. But
the toppings take it to the next level.
When you're picking out your toppings,
think about what might add new textures
(juicy tomatoes! crispy bacon!), flavors
(spicy chili crisp!), or colors (pickled red
onions! fresh herbs!).

Be sure to use small, dark-colored Hass
avocados for your toast—they have a
rich flavor and buttery texture. Larger,
bright-green Florida or "skinny" avocados
are too watery for this recipe; save them
for salads.

CONGEE

(Chinese Rice Porridge)

BEFORE YOU BEGIN

▶ Jasmine rice can be substituted for conventional long-grain white rice; do not use basmati rice.

▶ We prefer the distinctive flavor of Chinese black vinegar here; look for it with other Chinese ingredients at the supermarket or in Chinese markets.

"It had a really great texture and was super customizable."
—*Brenna, 17*

PREPARE INGREDIENTS

½ cup long-grain white rice

6 cups water

⅔ cup chicken broth

½ teaspoon salt

Scallions, root ends trimmed and scallions sliced thin

Fresh cilantro leaves

Unsalted dry-roasted peanuts, chopped coarse

Chili oil or toasted sesame oil

Chinese black vinegar or soy sauce

Jammy Eggs (optional) (see right)

JAMMY EGGS

These easy-to-make eggs have a consistency between a runny, soft-cooked egg and a fully set, hard-cooked egg. We love them on top of congee or a bowl of ramen (see page 98).

1–6 large eggs

In medium saucepan, bring ½ inch water to boil over medium-high heat. Use tongs to gently place up to 6 eggs in saucepan (eggs will not be submerged). Cover saucepan with lid and cook for 8 minutes. Transfer saucepan to sink and run cold water over eggs for 30 seconds to stop cooking. Peel eggs and discard shells. Use knife to slice eggs in half to serve.

START COOKING!

1. Set fine-mesh strainer over large bowl and set in sink. Place rice in strainer and rinse under cold running water, emptying bowl a few times as it fills, until water in bowl is clear, 1½ to 2 minutes. Shake strainer to drain rice well, then transfer rice to large saucepan. Discard water in bowl.

2. Add water, broth, and salt to saucepan. Bring to boil over high heat, stirring occasionally with wooden spoon.

3. Reduce heat to medium to keep mixture at vigorous simmer (small bubbles should break constantly and rapidly across surface of mixture). Cover saucepan with lid, tucking spoon horizontally between saucepan and lid to hold lid ajar. Cook at vigorous simmer, stirring occasionally, until mixture is thickened, glossy, and reduced by half, 45 to 50 minutes. Turn off heat.

4. Serve congee in bowls, passing scallions, cilantro, peanuts, oil, vinegar, and Jammy Eggs (if using) separately.

CONGEE: COMFORT FOOD WITH HISTORY

Filling, simple to prepare, and economical, porridge can be found in cuisines around the world. Like oatmeal is to Scotland and polenta to Italy, congee, a rice porridge, has been a staple in Chinese cooking for thousands of years.

"Congee" (borrowed from the Tamil term "kanji") is a generic term for the dish—it goes by different names and is prepared in different ways depending on the region. In Southern China, they serve a thicker style of congee, while elsewhere you may encounter a light, thin congee often served with savory toppings. Regardless of the style, congee is the best kind of comfort food: simple, homey, and perfect for eating on chilly mornings.

BEGINNER

VEGETARIAN

ACAI SMOOTHIE BOWLS

BEFORE YOU BEGIN

▶ Do not use Greek yogurt in this recipe, as it will make the smoothie bowls too thick.

▶ If you can't find frozen acai puree, you can increase the frozen mixed berries to 1¾ cups (8¾ ounces) and add 2 tablespoons of acai powder along with the other ingredients in step 3.

"My family liked it so much I made eight bowls of it!"
—Zev, 15

PREPARE INGREDIENTS

1 (3½-ounce) pouch unsweetened frozen acai puree

1 cup (5 ounces) frozen mixed berries

1 cup (5 ounces) frozen mango chunks

1 ripe banana, peeled and broken into pieces

½ cup plain yogurt

1 tablespoon honey

⅛ teaspoon salt

Toppings (see Up Your Game, right)

START COOKING!

1. Fill medium bowl with warm water. Place frozen acai pouch in water and thaw slightly, about 2 minutes.

2. Open pouch and add acai puree to food processor, breaking apart any large pieces. Add berries and mango and lock lid into place. Pulse until fruit is finely chopped, about twenty 1-second pulses.

3. Scrape down sides of processor bowl with rubber spatula. Add banana, yogurt, honey, and salt. Process until smooth, about 1 minute, stopping halfway through to scrape down sides of processor bowl.

4. Remove lid and carefully remove processor blade. Divide smoothie between 2 serving bowls. Add your favorite toppings. Serve.

▶ ▶ ▶ *UP YOUR GAME*

You can arrange fresh, crunchy, and sweet toppings in patterns on top of your smoothie base to create visual and textural contrast. Try some of these ideas:

Fresh Toppings: **blueberries**, **raspberries**, **blackberries**; sliced **strawberries**, **bananas**, **peaches**, or **kiwi**; chunks of fresh **mango** or **pineapple**

Crunchy Toppings: **granola**, **pepitas**, **sunflower seeds**, sliced **almonds**, **chia seeds**, **flaxseeds**

Sweet Toppings: shredded **coconut** or **coconut chips**; a drizzle of **honey** or **maple syrup**

WHAT IS ACAI?

Acai berries have been growing in the Amazon rain forest of Brazil for thousands of years but have only recently become widespread in the United States, popping up in smoothie shops and cafés from coast to coast. The deep-purple berries taste kind of like blueberries and are about the size of grapes. They have a very short shelf life and don't ship well, so they are generally sold in packets of frozen puree or in powder form. The frozen puree blends into a vivid purple smoothie bowl base that's made thick with the help of a food processor rather than a blender. Think of it as a blank canvas for making your colorful toppings pop.

STICKY BUNS

BEFORE YOU BEGIN

▶ For dough that is easy to work with and produces light, fluffy buns, we strongly recommend using a kitchen scale to weigh the flour and milk for the dough.

▶ Bake these buns in a metal baking pan (not glass or ceramic).

▶ We like the flavor and color of dark corn syrup here, but light corn syrup can be used instead.

PREPARE INGREDIENTS

FLOUR PASTE

⅔ cup (5⅓ ounces) milk

¼ cup (1¼ ounces) all-purpose flour

DOUGH

⅔ cup (5⅓ ounces) milk

1 large egg plus 1 large egg yolk
   (see page 191)

2¼ teaspoons instant or rapid-rise yeast

3¼ cups (16¼ ounces) all-purpose flour,
   plus extra for counter

3 tablespoons granulated sugar

1½ teaspoons salt

6 tablespoons unsalted butter, cut into
   6 pieces and softened

   Vegetable oil spray

TOPPING

¼ cup dark corn syrup

½ cup packed (3½ ounces) dark brown sugar

6 tablespoons unsalted butter, melted

¼ cup (1¾ ounces) granulated sugar

¼ teaspoon salt

2 tablespoons water

1 cup pecans, chopped (optional)

FILLING

1 teaspoon ground cinnamon

¾ cup packed (5¼ ounces) dark brown sugar

START COOKING!

1. For the flour paste: In small microwave-safe bowl, whisk ⅔ cup milk and ¼ cup flour until no lumps remain. Microwave, whisking every 20 to 30 seconds, until mixture thickens into pudding-like consistency, 50 to 90 seconds.

2. For the dough: Use rubber spatula to scrape flour paste into bowl of stand mixer. Add ⅔ cup milk and whisk until smooth. Add egg and egg yolk and whisk until incorporated. Add yeast and 3¼ cups flour. Lock bowl into place and attach dough hook to stand mixer.

3. Mix on low speed until no dry flour remains, about 2 minutes. Cover bowl with plastic wrap and let dough sit for 15 minutes.

4. Add 3 tablespoons granulated sugar and 1½ teaspoons salt to mixer bowl. Knead on medium-low speed for 5 minutes.

5. Add 6 tablespoons softened butter to mixer bowl and continue to knead on medium-low speed for 5 minutes, stopping mixer and scraping down dough hook and bowl halfway through kneading.

6. Sprinkle clean counter with extra flour and flour your hands. Scrape dough onto floured counter and use your floured hands to knead dough for 30 seconds. Move dough to clean portion of counter and form dough into smooth ball.

7. Spray large bowl with vegetable oil spray. Place dough in greased bowl and cover with plastic. Let dough rise until doubled in size, about 1 hour.

keep going >>>

8. For the topping: While dough rises, spray 13-by-9-inch metal baking pan with vegetable oil spray. In medium bowl, whisk corn syrup, ½ cup brown sugar, 6 tablespoons melted butter, ¼ cup granulated sugar, and ¼ teaspoon salt until smooth. Add water and whisk until incorporated. Pour mixture into greased baking pan and tilt pan to cover bottom. Sprinkle chopped pecans (if using) evenly over corn syrup mixture. Set aside.

9. For the filling: In small bowl, stir cinnamon and ¾ cup brown sugar until thoroughly combined; set aside.

10. When dough is ready, transfer to lightly floured counter (don't use too much flour—the dough needs to stick to the counter a bit as you shape it). Shape dough into buns, following photos, right.

11. Cover pan tightly with plastic and let rise until buns are puffy and touching one another, about 1 hour.

12. While buns rise, adjust oven racks to lowest and lower-middle positions. Place rimmed baking sheet on lowest rack (to catch any drips) and heat oven to 375 degrees.

13. When buns are ready, remove plastic. Bake buns on lower-middle rack until golden brown, 20 to 25 minutes.

14. Carefully place sheet of aluminum foil loosely on top of baking pan. Continue to bake for 15 minutes (or until buns register at least 200 degrees on instant-read thermometer).

15. Use oven mitts to transfer baking pan to cooling rack. Remove foil and let buns cool in baking pan for 5 minutes.

16. Place second rimmed baking sheet over buns. Holding baking pan with oven mitts, carefully flip buns upside down onto baking sheet. Remove baking pan and let buns cool for at least 15 minutes before serving. (Buns can be stored in airtight container for up to 2 days; microwave for 15 to 30 seconds before serving.)

MAKE STICKY BUNS IN TIME FOR BREAKFAST

This recipe takes about 4 hours to make, start to finish. If you want to serve your sticky buns at breakfast but don't want to get up quite so early, you can shape them the day before and bake them the next morning. After placing the buns in the pan in step 10, cover the pan tightly with plastic wrap and transfer it to the refrigerator for up to 18 hours. To bake, remove the baking pan from the refrigerator and let the buns sit until they are puffy and touching one another, 1½ to 2 hours, then proceed with step 12.

TAKING THE STICKY OUT OF STICKY BUNS

The ideal sticky bun features soft, fluffy bread; a spiral of gooey filling; and a sticky caramel glaze on top. But in the glaze is where the stickiness should stay. First things first: The more moisture in a bread dough, the fluffier it bakes up—and the stickier it is to work with. To combat this conundrum in our sticky bun dough, we use a Japanese baking technique commonly called by its Chinese name, tangzhong. For tangzhong, you cook a portion of the flour and liquid (milk, in this recipe) until it forms a pudding-like gel. The gel traps moisture inside of it—but doesn't make the dough wet or sticky when it's incorporated with the other ingredients. All the extra liquid trapped in the gel converts to steam during baking, making the buns light and fluffy.

HOW TO SHAPE STICKY BUNS

1. Press down on dough gently to deflate. Working from center toward edge, pat and stretch dough to form 18-by-15-inch rectangle with long side parallel to counter edge.

2. Sprinkle filling over dough, leaving 1-inch border along top edge. Use your hands to smooth filling into even layer, then gently press mixture into dough to stick.

3. Beginning with long edge nearest you, roll dough into log, taking care not to roll too tightly. Pinch seam to seal and roll log seam side down.

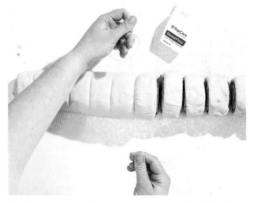

4. Use ruler and bench scraper or chef's knife to mark top of dough every 1½ inches (do not slice through dough). Hold long strand of dental floss tight and slide underneath dough log, stopping at first mark. Cross ends of floss over each other and pull to slice dough into portion. Transfer bun, cut side down, onto topping mixture in pan. Repeat with remaining dough, making 12 equal portions, spacing buns evenly apart in 4 rows of 3 buns.

OVERNIGHT ENGLISH MUFFINS

BEFORE YOU BEGIN

▶ This is a two-day project.

▶ If you have a kitchen scale, use it to weigh the dough into eight equal 2½-ounce portions in step 7.

PREPARE INGREDIENTS

2¼ cups (11¼ ounces) all-purpose flour, plus extra for counter

2 teaspoons instant or rapid-rise yeast

1¼ teaspoons salt

⅔ cup (5⅓ ounces) room-temperature whole milk

⅓ cup (2⅔ ounces) room-temperature water

1 tablespoon unsalted butter, melted

2 teaspoons sugar

Vegetable oil spray

2 tablespoons plus 2 tablespoons cornmeal, measured separately

---

HOW TO FOLD DOUGH

Spray your fingertips lightly with vegetable oil spray. Use your greased fingertips to fold dough over itself by gently lifting and folding edge of dough toward middle. Turn bowl 90 degrees and fold dough again; repeat turning bowl and folding dough 2 more times (for a total of 4 folds).

START COOKING!

DAY 1

1. In bowl of stand mixer, whisk together flour, yeast, and salt. Lock bowl into place and attach dough hook to stand mixer. In 4-cup liquid measuring cup, whisk milk, water, melted butter, and sugar until sugar has dissolved.

2. With mixer running on low speed, slowly pour milk mixture into flour mixture and mix until no dry flour is visible, about 2 minutes. Increase speed to medium-low and knead dough for 8 minutes.

3. Spray large bowl with vegetable oil spray. Use rubber spatula to scrape dough into greased bowl. Cover bowl with plastic wrap. Let dough rise on counter for 30 minutes.

4. Spray your fingertips lightly with vegetable oil spray. Fold dough 4 times following photo, left, turning bowl 90 degrees in between each fold.

5. Re-cover bowl tightly with plastic and let dough rise until doubled in size, 30 minutes to 1 hour.

6. Sprinkle 2 tablespoons cornmeal over rimmed baking sheet. Remove plastic from bowl. Press down on dough to deflate. Sprinkle clean counter with extra flour. Transfer dough to floured counter and gently pat into rectangle.

7. Use bench scraper or chef's knife to divide dough into 8 equal pieces (about 2½ ounces each). Spray large piece of plastic with vegetable oil spray. Cover dough with greased plastic.

8. Working with 1 piece of dough at a time, shape dough into balls, place on cornmeal-covered baking sheet, cover with greased plastic, and top with second rimmed baking sheet following photos, page 47. Let dough balls rise on counter for 30 minutes.

9. Refrigerate dough (still sandwiched between baking sheets) for at least 12 hours or up to 24 hours.

keep going >>>

DAY 2

10. When ready to cook muffins, remove baking sheets from refrigerator. Remove top baking sheet and loosen plastic covering muffins, but keep them covered (some muffins may develop large air bubbles as they rise; do not pop them). Let muffins sit at room temperature for 1 hour.

11. Adjust oven rack to lower-middle position and heat oven to 350 degrees. Remove plastic and sprinkle muffins with remaining 2 tablespoons cornmeal. Use your hands to gently press cornmeal into surface of muffins.

12. Heat 12-inch skillet over medium heat for 2 minutes.

13. Use spatula to carefully place 4 muffins in skillet. Cook until puffed and well browned on first side, 3 to 6 minutes (do not press down on muffins). Flip muffins and cook until well browned on second side, 2 to 4 minutes.

14. Transfer muffins to clean baking sheet. Repeat cooking with remaining 4 muffins. (If cornmeal in skillet starts to burn, use paper towel to carefully wipe out excess.)

15. Transfer baking sheet to oven and bake muffins until sides are firm (or muffins register 205 to 210 degrees on instant-read thermometer), about 10 minutes.

16. Use oven mitts to transfer baking sheet to cooling rack. Let muffins cool on baking sheet for 15 minutes. To split muffin open, turn muffin on its side, then poke tip of fork gently around edge of muffin. Toast muffins before serving.

A BREAKFAST WORTH THE WAIT

These English muffins are a two-day project, but they're well worth the wait. Letting the shaped dough balls rise in the refrigerator overnight (or for up to a full day) gives the yeast plenty of time to get to work. During that long stint in the fridge, the yeast slowly consumes sugars in the dough and creates lots of complex-tasting flavor compounds. The yeast also produces carbon dioxide gas, forming bubbles in the dough and causing it to rise—but not too much. The weight of the rimmed baking sheet on top of the dough forces it into that classic English muffin shape. And those gas bubbles? In the oven they'll turn into nooks and crannies, ready to hold your butter, jam, or peanut butter.

"The end result was amazing and was definitely worth all of the waiting!"
—Claire, 13

HOW TO SHAPE ENGLISH MUFFINS

1. Working with 1 piece of dough at a time, on clean counter, use your hands to fold corners of dough into center and pinch edges together (keep remaining pieces covered).

2. Flip dough. Use your cupped hand to drag ball in small circles until top feels tight. Repeat with remaining pieces of dough.

3. Place dough balls, seam side down, on cornmeal-covered baking sheet, leaving space between balls.

4. Spray extra-large piece of plastic wrap with vegetable oil spray. Cover baking sheet loosely with greased plastic. Gently place second rimmed baking sheet on top.

chapter 2
SNACKS

PARTY MIX

BEFORE YOU BEGIN

▶ You can use rice, corn, or wheat Chex cereal for this recipe.

"A more refined version of standard party mix."
—Roan, 14

PREPARE INGREDIENTS

Vegetable oil spray

4 cups Chex cereal

1 cup mini pretzels

1 cup pita chips, broken into 1-inch pieces

1 cup dry-roasted peanuts

1 cup popped popcorn

6 tablespoons unsalted butter, melted

3 tablespoons Worcestershire sauce

1 teaspoon garlic powder

START COOKING!

1. Adjust oven rack to middle position and heat oven to 250 degrees. Spray rimmed baking sheet with vegetable oil spray.

2. In large bowl, combine cereal, mini pretzels, pita chips, peanuts, and popcorn. Use rubber spatula to stir to combine.

3. In small bowl, whisk together melted butter, Worcestershire, and garlic powder. Drizzle mixture over cereal mix in large bowl. Stir until cereal mix is evenly coated with sauce.

4. Transfer mixture to greased baking sheet. Spread into even layer. Bake mixture until golden brown and crisp, about 45 minutes.

5. Use oven mitts to transfer baking sheet to cooling rack and let mixture cool completely, about 20 minutes. Serve. (Party Mix can be stored in airtight container at room temperature for up to 1 week.)

PARTY MIX AND TV: A DELICIOUS DUO

"TV mixes" got their start in the 1950s, when televisions were first becoming popular in American households and families were looking for something to munch on while watching their favorite shows. In 1952, an ad for Chex cereal in *LIFE* magazine featured a recipe for TV mix—a buttery mix of Chex cereal and nuts—and an iconic snack food was born. (Packaged Chex Mix wasn't sold until 1985.)

While the store-bought stuff might be convenient, we're firm believers in going the homemade route. Tossing the crunchy ingredients with melted butter adds a bit of richness but doesn't make things greasy. And adding savory Worcestershire sauce and garlic powder to the melted butter ensures that every piece of Party Mix is thoroughly coated in flavor.

▶ ▶ ▶ UP YOUR GAME

BBQ Party Mix: Reduce melted butter to 2 tablespoons. Omit Worcestershire sauce and garlic powder. In step 3, whisk ¼ cup **barbecue sauce**, 1 teaspoon **chili powder**, ½ teaspoon **dried oregano**, ¼ teaspoon **salt**, and ⅛ teaspoon **cayenne pepper** (optional) with melted butter.

Soy-Ginger Party Mix: Omit Worcestershire sauce and reduce garlic powder to ¾ teaspoon. In step 3, whisk 2 tablespoons **soy sauce**, 1 teaspoon **ground ginger**, and ⅛ teaspoon **cayenne pepper** (optional) with melted butter and garlic powder.

MAKES 16 BITES / 15 MINUTES
plus chilling time

CHOCOLATE-CHERRY ENERGY BITES

BEFORE YOU BEGIN

▶ You can add 1 tablespoon of chia seeds or ground flaxseeds to the oat mixture in step 1, if desired.

"It was pretty simple to make, and ended up as a really good snack. I really liked it!"
—Luccia, 14

PREPARE INGREDIENTS

¾ cup (2¼ ounces) old-fashioned rolled oats

⅓ cup (2 ounces) semisweet chocolate chips

⅓ cup pecans, chopped

⅓ cup dried cherries, chopped

⅓ cup creamy peanut, almond, or sunflower butter

2 tablespoons honey

⅛ teaspoon salt

START COOKING!

1. Add all ingredients to large bowl. Use rubber spatula to stir until well combined.

2. Use your wet hands to roll mixture into 16 balls (about 1 tablespoon each). Place balls on large plate and cover with plastic wrap.

3. Place in refrigerator and chill until bites are firm, at least 30 minutes or up to 3 days. Serve. (Bites can be refrigerated in airtight container for up to 3 days.)

▶ ▶ ▶ *UP YOUR GAME*

You can customize your energy bites by swapping in your favorite nuts and dried fruit. Try chopped **pistachios**, **cashews**, **almonds**, or **walnuts** in place of the pecans. **Dried cranberries**, **dried blueberries**, or **raisins** can be substituted for the dried cherries. You can also use **white chocolate chips** instead of semisweet.

A BIG BOOST IN A TINY BITE

These sweet, crunchy, chewy, bites are perfect for a quick snack on-the-go. They pack a lot of power into a tiny package: The nuts and nut butter provide protein and fat, the dried fruit adds some sugar, and the oats bring complex carbohydrates. The sugar gives you a fast-acting (but short-lived) energy boost, while the complex carbs, protein, and fat help keep you feeling full for longer.

BEGINNER

VEGETARIAN

BLISTERED SHISHITO PEPPERS

BEFORE YOU BEGIN

▶ You can season these peppers with flake sea salt, kosher salt, or a flavored salt.

"Super simple and delicious, and a bit daring!"
—Justin, 17

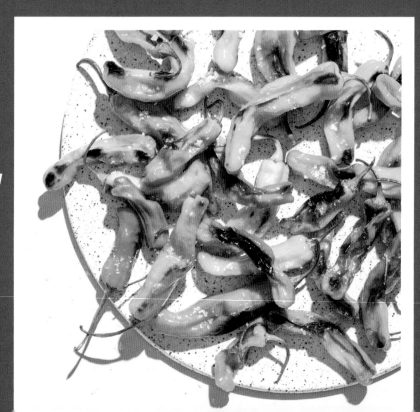

PREPARE INGREDIENTS

2 teaspoons vegetable oil

8 ounces shishito peppers

Flake sea salt

START COOKING!

1. In 12-inch nonstick skillet, heat oil over medium-high heat until just beginning to smoke, about 3 minutes. (You should start to see wisps of smoke coming up from oil; you may need to get eye level with skillet to see this. Turn on your stove's vent hood, if you have one.)

2. Carefully add peppers and place lid on skillet, leaving lid slightly ajar (see photo, right). Cook peppers, without stirring, until skins are blistered, 3 to 5 minutes (stand back from skillet—oil will pop!).

3. Turn off heat and slide skillet to cool burner. Use oven mitts to remove lid. Use tongs to flip peppers; replace lid, leaving lid slightly ajar. Continue to cook over medium-high heat until blistered on second side, 3 to 5 minutes. Turn off heat.

4. Transfer peppers to serving bowl. Season with flake sea salt to taste (see page 15). Let cool for 5 minutes before serving.

WHY LEAVE THE LID AJAR

When cooking the peppers, keeping the skillet almost—but not all the way—covered with the lid helps keep the oil from splattering out of the skillet.

Carefully add peppers and place lid on skillet slightly to one side (ajar), leaving small gap but keeping skillet mostly covered.

SHISHITO PEPPERS 101

These wrinkly-skinned green peppers originally hail from Japan, though their growing popularity in the United States has made it easier to find them in supermarkets, not just at restaurants. They're often fried in a tempura batter or blistered in a skillet, as they are in this recipe, and sometimes served with a dipping sauce.

Shishitos taste sweet and earthy, but not spicy. On the Scoville scale (the scale on which chile heat is measured), they're rated as very mild. They're hotter than bell peppers but fall far below jalapeño chiles. But be forewarned: About one in every 10 shishitos packs some heat, which adds a hint of suspense to every bite.

BUFFALO CHICKEN DIP

BEFORE YOU BEGIN

▶ Serve with tortilla chips, carrot sticks, and/or celery sticks.

"I like that it's creamy and super easy to make."
—Elly, 15

PREPARE INGREDIENTS

- 8 ounces cream cheese, cut into 8 pieces
- ⅓ cup Frank's hot sauce (or other not-too-spicy hot sauce)
- 1½ cups shredded rotisserie or leftover chicken
- ½ cup ranch dressing
- 1 teaspoon Worcestershire sauce
- ½ cup (2 ounces) plus 2 tablespoons crumbled blue cheese, measured separately
- ½ cup shredded sharp cheddar cheese (2 ounces)
- 1 scallion, root end trimmed and scallion sliced thin

START COOKING!

1. Adjust oven rack to middle position and heat oven to 350 degrees.

2. In medium microwave-safe bowl, add cream cheese and hot sauce. Microwave mixture for 2 minutes. Remove from microwave and whisk until smooth and no lumps remain.

3. Add chicken, ranch dressing, Worcestershire, and ½ cup blue cheese to bowl. Use rubber spatula to stir mixture until just combined. Transfer mixture to 9-inch pie plate or 8-inch square baking dish.

4. Bake dip for 10 minutes. Use oven mitts to transfer pie plate to cooling rack. Sprinkle cheddar evenly over top.

5. Continue to bake until cheddar is melted and dip is bubbling around edges, about 10 minutes.

6. Transfer pie plate to cooling rack and let cool for 5 minutes. Sprinkle with scallion and remaining 2 tablespoons blue cheese. Serve.

FROM WINGS TO DIP

This scoopable dip features all the things that make buffalo wings so irresistible—tender chicken, spicy hot sauce, creamy ranch dressing, and tangy blue cheese. While wings were the first thing on the buffalo bandwagon, that iconic buffalo flavor has since made its way onto everything from pizza to cauliflower to dip.

But who gets credit for creating the original buffalo wings? Most people believe that title belongs to Teressa Bellissimo, co-owner of Anchor Bar in Buffalo, New York, who, in 1964, allegedly cut up some chicken wings, fried them, doused them in a spicy mystery sauce, and served them with blue cheese dressing.

Many others believe John Young, then-owner of John Young's Wings & Things (also in Buffalo) is the actual inventor. In 1963, Young started selling his wings, fried whole (instead of the two smaller pieces you normally see) and topped with mumbo sauce, a spicy tomato-based condiment. While buffalo wings' origin story remains a mystery, their spicy flavor lives on.

BEGINNER

VEGETARIAN

PAJEON

(Korean Scallion Pancake)

BEFORE YOU BEGIN

▶ Gochugaru is a type of Korean chile flake; be sure to use the coarse variety, sometimes labeled "coarse powder." If you can't find gochugaru, substitute ⅛ to ¼ teaspoon of red pepper flakes.

▶ Potato starch is available in Asian markets and some supermarkets and creates the crispiest pancake. If can't find it, you can substitute cornstarch, but your pancake will be softer and less crisp.

RECIPE FOR A RAINY DAY

Jeon are savory, crispy Korean pancakes that can be made with a wide array of ingredients. Pajeon ("pa" means "scallions" in Korean) is one of the most popular varieties, featuring a crispy, browned exterior and a soft, chewy interior that's packed with oniony scallions. In Korea, pajeon is a particularly popular snack on rainy days: Some say that the sputter and sizzle of the pajeon batter cooking in oil sounds like the rhythmic tapping of rainfall.

PREPARE INGREDIENTS

DIPPING SAUCE

2	tablespoons soy sauce
1	tablespoon water
2	teaspoons unseasoned rice vinegar
1	teaspoon toasted sesame oil
½–1	teaspoon gochugaru
½	teaspoon sugar

PANCAKE

5	scallions, root ends trimmed
½	cup all-purpose flour
2	tablespoons potato starch
½	teaspoon baking powder
⅛	teaspoon baking soda
¼	teaspoon pepper
⅛	teaspoon salt
½	teaspoon sugar
½	cup ice water (see page 12)
1	garlic clove, peeled and minced (see page 13)
2	tablespoons plus 1 tablespoon vegetable oil, measured separately

---

▶ ▶ ▶ **UP YOUR GAME**

Instead of scallions, try using 1 cup of chopped **baby greens** (such as **kale**, **arugula**, or **spinach**), 1 cup of sliced **mushrooms**, or ½ cup of chopped **kimchi**.

START COOKING!

1. For the dipping sauce: In small bowl, whisk together all dipping sauce ingredients.

2. For the pancake: Line large plate with double layer of paper towels. Place scallions on cutting board. Use chef's knife to cut dark-green scallion tops from white and light-green bottoms. Cut white and light-green parts in half lengthwise (the long way; skip this step if your scallions are skinny). Cut all scallion parts crosswise (the short way) into 2-inch pieces.

3. In medium bowl, whisk together flour, potato starch, baking powder, baking soda, pepper, salt, and ½ teaspoon sugar. Add ice water and garlic and whisk until smooth. Use rubber spatula to gently stir in scallions until mixture is evenly combined (do not overmix; see page 15).

4. In 10-inch nonstick skillet, heat 2 tablespoons oil over medium-high heat until just beginning to smoke, about 3 minutes. (You should start to see wisps of smoke coming up from oil; you may need to get eye level with skillet to see this. Turn on your stove's vent hood, if you have one.) Scrape all of batter into center of skillet. Spread into even circle covering bottom of skillet. Shake skillet to distribute oil under pancake.

5. Cook until bubbles at center of pancake burst and leave holes in surface and underside is golden brown, 3 to 5 minutes. (Oil should be gently sizzling as pancake cooks; if oil begins to smoke, reduce heat to medium.)

6. Use spatula to flip pancake and press firmly into skillet to flatten. Drizzle remaining 1 tablespoon oil around edges of skillet. Continue to cook, pressing pancake occasionally to flatten, until second side is spotty golden brown, 2 to 4 minutes. Turn off heat.

7. Transfer pancake to paper towel–lined plate. Let drain and cool for 5 minutes. Transfer pancake to cutting board and cut into 6 wedges. Serve with dipping sauce.

INTERMEDIATE

VEGETARIAN

ONIGIRI

(Japanese Rice Balls)

BEFORE YOU BEGIN

▶ If you have an onigiri rice mold, you can use it to shape the rice balls into triangles in step 6 instead of shaping them by hand.

▶ You can choose to make one filling for all your onigiri or make a few fillings.

"It was wonderful! The Tuna-Mayo Filling was absolutely delicious."
—Lauren, 17

PREPARE INGREDIENTS

1¼ cups sushi rice

1½ cups water

¼ teaspoon salt

1 (8-by-7½-inch) sheet nori

1 recipe onigiri filling (see below)

White or black sesame seeds,
raw or toasted (optional)

ONIGIRI FILLINGS

Many onigiri have a little bit of intensely
flavored filling hidden inside. Try making
one or more of these fillings for your onigiri.

Tuna-Mayo Filling: Stir together ¼ cup
drained canned tuna, 1 tablespoon
mayonnaise (Kewpie, a Japanese
brand, is great if you can find it!),
and ½ teaspoon soy sauce.

Okaka Filling: Stir together ½ cup bonito
flakes and 1 teaspoon soy sauce.

Ume Filling: Rinse ⅓ cup umeboshi
(Japanese salted, pickled plums) and pat
dry. Use fork to mash, then remove pits.
(Umeboshi are supersalty, so use only
½ teaspoon of this filling per onigiri.)

START COOKING!

1. Set fine-mesh strainer over large bowl and set
in sink. Place rice in strainer and rinse under cold
running water, emptying bowl a few times as it
fills, until water in bowl is clear, 1½ to 2 minutes.
Shake strainer to drain rice well and transfer to
medium saucepan.

2. Stir in water and salt. Bring rice to boil over
medium-high heat. Reduce heat to low, cover
saucepan with lid, and cook for 20 minutes.

3. Turn off heat and slide saucepan to cool
burner. Let rice sit, covered, for 10 minutes to
finish cooking.

4. While rice cooks and cools, use kitchen shears
to cut three 1-inch-wide strips from nori sheet.
Cut strips in half crosswise (the short way; you'll
have 6 pieces total). Set aside. Prepare your
choice of filling (see left).

5. Rinse and dry now-empty large bowl. Use
rubber spatula to transfer cooked rice to bowl. Let
cool until easy to handle but still very warm, about
5 minutes.

6. Line ½-cup dry measuring cup with plastic
wrap. Fill and shape onigiri following photos,
page 62. Repeat with remaining rice and filling
to make 6 onigiri total.

7. Sprinkle outsides of onigiri with sesame
seeds (if using). Serve. (Onigiri can be wrapped
individually in plastic wrap and refrigerated in
airtight container for up to 24 hours.)

keep going >>>

HOW TO FILL AND SHAPE ONIGIRI

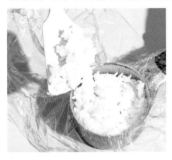

1. Use rubber spatula and your damp hands to fill plastic-lined measuring cup with warm rice.

2. Use back of 1-teaspoon measuring spoon to make indentation in center of rice. Add 1 teaspoon filling (½ teaspoon if using Ume Filling) to indentation. Place 1 teaspoon rice on top of filling.

3. Gather edges of plastic together; lift out of measuring cup; and twist and gently squeeze to form rice into ball, enclosing filling inside.

4. Use your hands to gently flatten ball on counter into disk about 1 inch thick. Turn disk onto edge and press to flatten. Rotate and flatten edges a few times to shape into triangle. Triangle should measure about 3 inches long on each side and about 1 inch thick.

5. Unwrap rice triangle and place 1 end of 1 nori strip in center of triangle. Wrap nori around 1 edge to other side, pressing lightly to adhere (this gives you a place to hold the onigiri when eating without getting your fingers sticky).

6. Place onigiri on serving plate and return plastic to measuring cup. Use ¼-teaspoon measuring spoon to top onigiri with ¼ teaspoon filling.

ONIGIRI ON THE GO

Onigiri, also called omusubi, are a popular snack in Japan. They're made from sticky rice that's molded into shapes and wrapped with pieces of nori (a seaweed), which gives you a convenient spot to hold your onigiri. Triangles are the most common shape, but you'll also see onigiri circles, cylinders, or even adorable animal shapes. These savory, chewy snacks can be served plain, filled or mixed with flavorful ingredients, or brushed with a salty-sweet glaze and charcoal-grilled or pan-fried (a style called "yaki").

Some people make onigiri at home and add them to a bento lunch box, but they're also widely available at Japanese kiosks, food trucks, and convenience stores called conbini. Packaged onigiri come with a huge variety of fillings, from the traditional ones in this recipe to innovative flavors, such as fried chicken, Korean-style barbecued beef, tempura shrimp, or Spam. Filling and easy to eat (no utensils needed!), onigiri make a satisfying on-the-go snack for busy days.

PIZZA POCKETS

BEFORE YOU BEGIN

▶ You can substitute 30 regular-size pepperoni slices, cut into quarters, for the mini pepperoni slices.

CRISPY POCKETS (WITHOUT A SLEEVE)

You know the frozen savory hand pies from the grocery store—the ones that come with a special cardboard sleeve? That sleeve surrounds a thin film of metal that converts a microwave's electromagnetic energy into radiant heat, which keeps the crust crisp. We can't send you a sleeve, but luckily you won't need one.

This recipe's sturdy pastry contains the filling—but won't get soggy. The butter helps the dough bake up tender but crispy, and the egg wash helps with browning. When you reheat your pockets in the microwave, the crust stays crisp—no sleeve required!

PREPARE INGREDIENTS

3¼ cups (16¼ ounces) all-purpose flour, plus extra for counter

1 tablespoon sugar

1½ teaspoons salt

12 tablespoons unsalted butter, cut into 12 pieces and chilled

2 large eggs (1 whole, 1 lightly beaten with fork)

½ cup (4 ounces) ice water (see page 12)

⅓ cup jarred pizza sauce

½ cup (2 ounces) mini pepperoni slices

4 mozzarella cheese sticks, cut in half crosswise

▶ ▶ ▶ **UP YOUR GAME**

Broccoli and Cheddar Pockets: Omit pizza sauce. Substitute ½ cup finely chopped **broccoli florets** (defrosted if using frozen or cooked if using fresh) for pepperoni and 4 **cheddar cheese sticks** for mozzarella cheese sticks. When assembling pockets, add pinch **salt** and pinch **pepper** to each pocket.

Ham and Cheese Pockets: Omit pizza sauce. Substitute ½ cup finely chopped **deli ham** for pepperoni and 4 **cheddar cheese sticks** for mozzarella cheese sticks.

START COOKING!

1. Place flour, sugar, and salt in food processor. Lock lid into place. Process mixture for 3 seconds.

2. Sprinkle chilled butter pieces over flour mixture. Pulse until mixture looks like coarse crumbs, eight to ten 1-second pulses.

3. Add whole egg and ice water. Process until dough comes together into smooth ball, 30 to 45 seconds.

4. Remove lid and carefully remove processor blade. Sprinkle clean counter lightly with extra flour. Transfer dough to floured counter and press together into ball. Use bench scraper or chef's knife to divide dough in half.

5. Form each piece of dough into 5-inch square. Wrap each square tightly in plastic wrap. Refrigerate dough until chilled, at least 30 minutes or up to 24 hours.

6. Adjust oven rack to middle position and heat oven to 350 degrees. Line rimmed baking sheet with parchment paper.

7. Let chilled dough sit on counter to soften slightly before rolling, about 10 minutes.

8. Sprinkle counter lightly with extra flour. Roll, cut, fill, and shape dough to make 8 pizza pockets following photos, page 66.

9. Use pastry brush to paint tops and sides of pizza pockets lightly with beaten egg.

10. Bake pizza pockets until edges are just beginning to brown, 20 to 24 minutes.

11. Use oven mitts to transfer baking sheet to cooling rack. Let pizza pockets cool on baking sheet for 10 minutes before serving. (Pizza pockets can be frozen for up to 1 month. Transfer baked and cooled pockets to zipper-lock freezer bag, press out air, and seal bag. To serve, reheat pockets [do not thaw before reheating] in microwave for 1 to 2 minutes.)

keep going >>>

Rolling the dough for the tops of the pizza pockets slightly larger than the dough for the bottoms leaves enough dough to drape over the piled-up fillings.

1. Use rolling pin to roll 1 piece of dough into 10½-inch square on floured counter.

2. Use bench scraper or chef's knife to cut off edges of dough to form tidy 10-inch square. Cut dough into eight 2½-by-5-inch rectangles.

3. Place rectangles on parchment-lined baking sheet. (These will be the bottoms of your pockets.) Place baking sheet in refrigerator to chill.

4. Roll second piece of dough into 10½-by-12½-inch rectangle. Use bench scraper to cut off edges of dough to form tidy 10-by-12-inch rectangle. Cut dough into eight 3-by-5-inch rectangles. Use fork to poke 1 row of holes down center of each rectangle. (These will be the tops of your pockets.)

5. Remove baking sheet with bottoms from refrigerator. Use 1-teaspoon measuring spoon to spoon 2 teaspoons pizza sauce in center of each bottom rectangle. Top each with 2 heaping teaspoons mini pepperoni slices, followed by half a mozzarella cheese stick. Dip your finger in water and lightly moisten edges of each rectangle.

6. Place 1 top rectangle onto each bottom rectangle, making sure all edges are lined up. Use your fingers to firmly press edges of top and bottom edges of rectangles together to seal, then use fork to press sealed edges together to crimp dough.

Slice-and-Bake

CHEDDAR CRACKERS

BEFORE YOU BEGIN

▶ Yellow cheddar gives these crackers a nice orange color, but you can also use white cheddar.

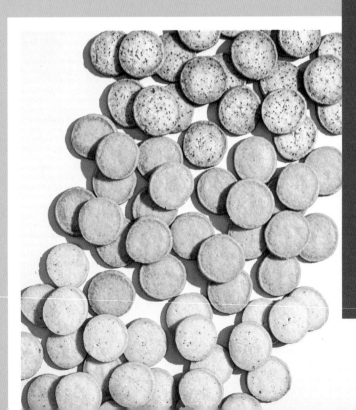

KEEPING CRACKERS IN SHAPE

These crackers keep their circular shapes due to a stint in the refrigerator. Chilling is key because of the butter in the cracker dough. Butter is solid and firm when it's cold, but it becomes softer as it warms up. As you mix the dough in the food processor, the butter heats up, making a soft dough that's easy to shape into a log. An hour in the fridge gives the butter time to firm up again and allows you to slice perfectly round (or at least roundish) crackers that keep their shape as they bake.

PREPARE INGREDIENTS

1 cup shredded yellow extra-sharp cheddar cheese (4 ounces)

¾ cup (3¾ ounces) all-purpose flour, plus extra for counter

4 tablespoons unsalted butter, cut into 4 pieces and chilled

1½ teaspoons cornstarch

¼ teaspoon salt

⅛ teaspoon paprika

Pinch cayenne pepper

1 tablespoon ice water

▶ ▶ ▶ **UP YOUR GAME**

Slice-and-Bake Everything Crackers:
Add 1 tablespoon **poppy seeds**,
1 teaspoon **sesame seeds**, ½ teaspoon
granulated garlic, and ½ teaspoon **onion flakes** to food processor along with flour in step 1.

Slice-and-Bake Cacio e Pepe Crackers:
Substitute ¾ cup shredded **Asiago** for cheddar. Omit paprika and cayenne. Add
½ cup grated **Pecorino Romano cheese** and ½ teaspoon **pepper** to food processor along with flour in step 1.

START COOKING!

1. Add cheddar, flour, chilled butter, cornstarch, salt, paprika, and cayenne to food processor and lock lid into place. Process until mixture looks like wet sand, about 20 seconds. Add ice water. Process until dough begins to clump together, 20 to 30 seconds.

2. Remove lid and carefully remove processor blade. Sprinkle clean counter lightly with flour. Transfer dough to floured counter; form into ball; and gently knead until smooth, about 15 seconds.

3. Use your hands to roll dough into even 10-inch-long log. Wrap dough tightly in plastic wrap. Place dough on plate and refrigerate until firm, about 1 hour. (Dough can be refrigerated for up to 3 days or frozen for up to 1 month.)

4. Adjust oven rack to middle position and heat oven to 350 degrees. Line rimmed baking sheet with parchment paper.

5. Unwrap chilled dough log and place on cutting board. Use chef's knife to slice dough ¼ inch thick and place on parchment-lined baking sheet (you should have about 36 crackers).

6. Bake crackers until light golden around edges, 20 to 25 minutes, using oven mitts to rotate baking sheet halfway through baking (see page 15).

7. Transfer baking sheet to cooling rack. Let crackers cool completely on baking sheet, about 30 minutes. Serve. (Crackers can be stored in airtight container at room temperature for up to 3 days.)

chapter 3
LUNCH

KALE CAESAR SALAD *with Chicken*

BEFORE YOU BEGIN

▶ The anchovy won't make your dressing taste fishy—it adds a savory umami boost.

MASSAGE YOUR KALE (REALLY!)
Squeezing and massaging sturdy kale leaves breaks down the kale's plant cells, leaving you with a tender (not chewy or tough) base for your salad.

"Tastes really good, the dressing was perfect— tangy and kinda sweet."
—Seth, 14

PREPARE INGREDIENTS

CROUTONS

2 ounces baguette, cut into ¾-inch cubes (about 2 cups)

1 tablespoon extra-virgin olive oil

Pinch salt

Pinch pepper

DRESSING

¼ cup mayonnaise

1½ tablespoons lemon juice, squeezed from 1 lemon

1 teaspoon Dijon mustard

1 teaspoon Worcestershire sauce

1 small garlic clove, peeled and minced (see page 13)

1 anchovy fillet, rinsed, patted dry, and minced

2 tablespoons grated Parmesan cheese

2 tablespoons extra-virgin olive oil

¼ teaspoon salt

⅛ teaspoon pepper

SALAD

8 ounces curly kale

1 cup shredded rotisserie or leftover chicken

¼ cup grated Parmesan cheese

START COOKING!

1. For the croutons: Adjust oven rack to middle position and heat oven to 350 degrees. In medium bowl, toss together all crouton ingredients. Transfer to rimmed baking sheet.

2. Bake until croutons are golden and crisp, about 15 minutes. Use oven mitts to transfer baking sheet to cooling rack. Let croutons cool completely, about 10 minutes.

3. For the dressing: In small bowl, whisk all dressing ingredients until well combined.

4. For the salad: On cutting board, remove kale leaves from stems (see photo, below). Use chef's knife to chop leaves into 1-inch pieces. Transfer leaves to large bowl. Squeeze and massage kale until leaves soften and turn dark green, 1 to 2 minutes.

5. Add dressing to kale and use tongs to toss until leaves are well coated. Add chicken, croutons, and ¼ cup Parmesan and toss to combine. Season with salt and pepper to taste (see page 15). Serve.

HOW TO STEM KALE

Hold end of kale stem in 1 hand. Pinch stem with thumb and index finger of other hand. Slide your hand down length of stem from bottom to top. Discard stem.

BLATS

(Bacon, Lettuce, Avocado, and Tomato Sandwiches)

BEFORE YOU BEGIN

▶ You can substitute your favorite type of lettuce for the Bibb lettuce.

"I really liked the little details, like the marinade for the tomatoes."
—Zoey, 14

PREPARE INGREDIENTS

4   slices cooked bacon (see below)

1   tablespoon extra-virgin olive oil

1½ teaspoons red wine vinegar

¼   teaspoon salt

¼   teaspoon pepper

1   ripe tomato, cored (see page 155) and cut into ¼-inch-thick slices

1   ripe avocado, halved and pitted (see page 14)

4   slices hearty sandwich bread, toasted

1   tablespoon mayonnaise

4   Bibb lettuce leaves

START COOKING!

1. In small bowl, use spoon to stir together oil, vinegar, salt, and pepper. Add tomato slices to bowl and gently stir to coat with dressing.

2. Scoop avocado halves out of skins into second small bowl. Discard skins. Use fork to roughly mash avocado.

3. Place toast on cutting board. Use knife to spread mayonnaise evenly over 2 slices of toast. Spread mashed avocado evenly over remaining 2 slices of toast. Break bacon slices in half.

4. Distribute half of bacon over toast slices topped with mashed avocado, followed by half of lettuce. Top with tomato, remaining lettuce, and remaining bacon and cap with toast slices spread with mayonnaise. Cut sandwiches in half and serve.

HOW TO COOK BACON IN THE MICROWAVE

Cooking bacon in the microwave is an easy, hands-off method. The cooking time will vary depending on your microwave. The paper towels absorb the grease and keep the bacon from making a mess.

1–6   slices bacon

Place up to 6 slices of bacon between 2 layers of paper towels on microwave-safe plate. Microwave until bacon is crispy and golden brown, 4 to 6 minutes.

OUR BLAT TRULY STACKS UP

A BLAT may seem like a sandwich so simple that it doesn't need a recipe, but our version is engineered to give you maximum flavor and texture in every bite. Layering ultracrispy bacon and lightly crunchy Bibb lettuce on either side of the juicy marinated tomato slices keeps the toast from getting soggy, while mayo and mashed avocado are the creamy, savory "glues" that hold our sandwich together.

PORK MEATBALL SANDWICHES

with Pickled Vegetables and Herbs

BEFORE YOU BEGIN

▶ Maggi Seasoning is a savory flavor enhancer common in Vietnamese cooking. It can be found in the international aisle of many supermarkets.

PREPARE INGREDIENTS

PICKLED VEGETABLES

6 ounces daikon radish, peeled and shredded (about 1½ cups)

2 carrots, peeled and shredded (about 1 cup)

½ teaspoon plus 2 tablespoons sugar, measured separately

½ teaspoon plus ¼ teaspoon salt, measured separately

¼ cup distilled white vinegar

¼ cup water

MEATBALLS

1 pound ground pork

¼ cup chopped fresh cilantro (see page 13)

2 scallions, root ends trimmed and scallions sliced thin

1 tablespoon fish sauce

½ teaspoon pepper

½ teaspoon salt

SANDWICHES

¼ cup mayonnaise

2 teaspoons sriracha

4 Vietnamese-style baguettes, about 6 inches each (see note, page 78), split lengthwise and toasted

2 teaspoons Maggi Seasoning (optional)

½ cup fresh cilantro leaves

START COOKING!

1. For the pickled vegetables: Set colander in large bowl. Add daikon, carrots, ½ teaspoon sugar, and ½ teaspoon salt to colander and use rubber spatula to toss to combine. Let sit for 30 minutes to drain.

2. Meanwhile, in medium bowl, whisk together vinegar, water, remaining 2 tablespoons sugar, and remaining ¼ teaspoon salt. Set aside.

3. When vegetables are ready, use rubber spatula to press on vegetables to remove excess liquid. Add drained vegetables to vinegar mixture and toss to combine. Let sit on counter for 30 minutes. (Pickled vegetables can be covered and refrigerated for up to 1 week.)

4. For the meatballs: Meanwhile, in clean large bowl, combine all meatball ingredients. Use your hands to mix until well combined. Roll pork mixture into 16 meatballs (about 2 tablespoons each) and place in 12-inch nonstick skillet.

5. Cook over medium-high heat, using tongs to turn occasionally, until browned on all sides, about 10 minutes.

keep going >>>

6. Cover skillet with lid and continue to cook until meatballs register 160 degrees on instant-read thermometer (see page 10), about 4 minutes. Turn off heat and slide skillet to cool burner.

7. For the sandwiches: In small bowl, combine mayonnaise and sriracha. Use spoon to stir until well combined. Spread mayonnaise mixture evenly on cut sides of each baguette.

8. When pickled vegetables are ready, drain them in colander set in sink. Divide drained pickled vegetables evenly between baguette bottoms.

9. Top vegetables with 4 meatballs per sandwich, drizzle with Maggi Seasoning (if using), and sprinkle cilantro evenly over top. Cap with baguette tops and press down gently. Serve.

"The sweet juicy veggies helped balance the spicy flavor of the sauce and meatballs."
—Maria, 16

NOT YOUR AVERAGE SANDWICH

These flavor- and texture-packed sandwiches are inspired by Vietnamese banh mi. The term "banh mi" actually refers to two things: It means "bread" in Vietnamese, and it also refers to a variety of sandwich invented in Saigon in the early 20th century, during the era of French colonization. Featuring various combinations of pork, chicken, tofu, and even cold cuts; pickled vegetables; fresh herbs; creamy mayonnaise; and pâté, banh mi strike the perfect balance of flavors (savory, spicy, tangy, fresh) and textures (crispy, creamy, crunchy).

But the real star of the show just might be the bread. Banh mi are traditionally made on Vietnamese-style baguettes, which have a crisp exterior and a soft, pillowy interior. You can find these airy rolls at Vietnamese bakeries or Asian markets. If you find longer loaves, cut them crosswise (the short way) into 6-inch lengths for this recipe. If you can't find Vietnamese-style baguettes, you can substitute Cubano rolls, Mexican bolillo or telera rolls, or ciabatta rolls. Traditional French baguettes with a thicker crust and chewy interior do not work as well in this recipe.

AREPAS

BEFORE YOU BEGIN

▶ Masarepa is also known as harina precocida and masa al instante. Look for it in the Latin section of your grocery store or in Latin markets. Make sure to use white, not yellow, masarepa. Do not substitute masa harina for the masarepa—it will not work in this recipe.

"I liked that everything timed out to be done at the same time."
—Victoria, 15

PREPARE INGREDIENTS

- 1   cup (5 ounces) masarepa blanca
- ½   teaspoon salt
- ½   teaspoon baking powder
- 1   cup plus 2 tablespoons (9 ounces) warm water
- 2   tablespoons vegetable oil
- 1   recipe arepa filling (see page 82)

ALL ABOUT AREPAS

Arepas—round corn cakes, often served grilled—are common in lots of Latin American countries. In Venezuela, where they're especially popular, arepas are typically split in half and then filled with anything from savory shredded beef to crumbled cotija cheese to sweet plantains—kind of like a corn cake sandwich. For our arepas, we started with a traditional corn cake made from masarepa (a type of flour made from corn), and we added baking powder to give our arepas a slightly lighter texture. From there, we created two recipes for classic Venezuelan fillings (see page 82).

START COOKING!

1. Adjust oven rack to middle position and heat oven to 400 degrees. Set cooling rack inside rimmed baking sheet.

2. In medium bowl, whisk together masarepa, salt, and baking powder. Slowly add warm water and use rubber spatula to stir until combined. Let mixture sit until liquid is absorbed and dough is shapeable, about 20 to 30 minutes. (Now is a good time to make your filling—see page 82.)

3. Divide dough evenly into 4 portions (about ⅓ cup each). Use your hands to form dough into four 3-inch rounds, each about ½ inch thick (see photo, below). Place on large plate.

keep going >>>

HOW TO SHAPE AREPAS

Divide dough evenly into 4 portions (about ⅓ cup each). Use your hands to form dough into four 3-inch rounds, each about ½ inch thick.

4. In 12-inch nonstick skillet, heat oil over medium-high heat until shimmering, about 2 minutes (oil should be hot but not smoking). Use spatula to carefully transfer arepas to skillet. Cook until golden on first side, about 4 minutes. Flip arepas and cook until golden on second side, about 4 minutes. Turn off heat.

5. Transfer arepas to cooling rack set in rimmed baking sheet. Bake until cooked through, about 10 minutes.

6. Use oven mitts to transfer baking sheet to second cooling rack. Let arepas cool on baking sheet for 5 minutes.

7. Split arepas open with fork to create pocket (like a pita!). Use 1-tablespoon measuring spoon to fill each arepa with 3 tablespoons filling. Serve.

AREPA FILLINGS

Arepas can be filled with everything from cheese to eggs to pork and more! Try one of these traditional Venezuelan fillings.

DOMINO (BLACK BEAN AND CHEESE) FILLING

- 1 cup rinsed and drained black beans
- ½ cup shredded Monterey Jack cheese (2 ounces)
- 1 scallion, root end trimmed and scallion sliced thin
- 1 tablespoon minced fresh cilantro (see page 13)
- 2 teaspoons lime juice, squeezed from ½ lime
- ⅛ teaspoon salt
- ⅛ teaspoon pepper

In medium bowl, use potato masher or fork to mash beans until mostly broken down. Add Monterey Jack, scallion, cilantro, lime juice, salt, and pepper to bowl and use rubber spatula to stir to combine.

REINA PEPIADA (CHICKEN AND AVOCADO) FILLING

- ¾ cup shredded rotisserie or leftover chicken
- ½ avocado, pitted and cut into ½-inch pieces (see page 14)
- 1 scallion, root end trimmed and scallion sliced thin
- 1 tablespoon minced fresh cilantro (see page 13)
- 2 teaspoons lime juice, squeezed from ½ lime
- 1 garlic clove, peeled and minced (see page 13)
- 1 teaspoon hot sauce (optional)
- ¼ teaspoon salt
- ⅛ teaspoon pepper

In medium bowl, add all ingredients. Use rubber spatula to stir until well combined.

GỎI CUỐN

(Vietnamese Summer Rolls)

BEFORE YOU BEGIN

▶ If you can't find Thai basil, don't substitute other kinds of basil; increase the mint and cilantro leaves to ¾ cup each instead.

▶ A wooden surface will draw moisture away from the wrappers, so assemble the rolls directly on your counter or on a plastic cutting board. If part of the wrapper starts to dry out while you are forming the rolls, lightly wet it with your fingers.

"It took time and practice to fill and fold the rolls, but they were great when I finished."
—Declan, 15

PREPARE INGREDIENTS

PEANUT-HOISIN SAUCE

1   Thai chile, stemmed (see page 14)
    and sliced thin

1   garlic clove, peeled and minced
    (see page 13)

1   teaspoon kosher salt

⅔   cup water

⅓   cup creamy peanut butter

3   tablespoons hoisin sauce

2   tablespoons tomato paste

1   tablespoon distilled white vinegar

SUMMER ROLLS

2   quarts water

3   ounces rice vermicelli noodles

18 frozen peeled and deveined medium-large
    shrimp (31 to 40 per pound), thawed and
    tails removed

½   cup fresh mint leaves

½   cup fresh cilantro leaves and thin stems

½   cup Thai basil leaves

6   red or green leaf lettuce leaves

6   (8½-inch) round rice paper wrappers

2   scallions, root ends trimmed and scallions
    sliced thin

START COOKING!

1. For the peanut-hoisin sauce: Place chile, garlic, and salt on cutting board in small pile. Place 1 hand on handle of chef's knife and rest fingers of your other hand on top of blade. Chop mixture, using rocking motion and pivoting knife as you chop, until very finely minced.

2. Transfer chile mixture to medium bowl. Add water, peanut butter, hoisin, tomato paste, and vinegar and whisk until smooth. Set aside.

3. For the summer rolls: Set fine-mesh strainer over large bowl. In medium saucepan, bring 2 quarts water to boil. Add noodles and use tongs to stir to separate noodles. Cook until noodles are tender but not mushy, 3 to 4 minutes. Turn off heat and carefully slide saucepan to cool burner.

4. Use tongs to transfer noodles to strainer set over large bowl. Add shrimp to water remaining in pot and cover with lid. Let sit, off heat, until shrimp turn pink and opaque throughout, about 3 minutes.

5. Meanwhile, rinse noodles in fine-mesh strainer with cold water until cool. Shake strainer to drain noodles well, then spread noodles out on plate to dry.

keep going >>>

6. Drain shrimp in now-empty fine-mesh strainer and rinse with cold water until cool. Shake strainer to drain shrimp well, and transfer to second plate. Pat shrimp dry with paper towels.

7. Tear mint, cilantro, and Thai basil into 1-inch pieces and combine in second medium bowl. Tear thick ribs from bottoms of lettuce leaves; discard ribs and set aside leaves. Line serving platter with parchment paper. Arrange all filling ingredients on counter (you will need to work quickly when assembling the rolls).

8. Rinse now-empty large bowl and fill with cold water. Submerge 1 rice paper wrapper in water until wet on both sides, no longer than 2 seconds. Shake gently over bowl to remove excess water, then lay wrapper flat on clean counter (see photo, right). Let soften for about 1 minute (wrapper will be fairly stiff but will continue to soften as you assemble roll).

9. Fill and shape roll following photos, right. Transfer roll to parchment-lined serving platter, shrimp side up, and cover loosely with plastic wrap. Repeat with remaining wrappers and filling. Make sure completed rolls do not touch one another on platter and keep them covered loosely with plastic.

10. Serve rolls with peanut-hoisin sauce.

HOW TO REHYDRATE RICE PAPER WRAPPERS

A quick dip in cold water moistens the wrapper slowly, giving you time to work; once you've added your fillings, the wrapper will be stretchy enough to roll but not so fragile that it tears.

Submerge 1 rice paper wrapper in cold water until wet on both sides, no longer than 2 seconds. Shake gently over bowl to remove excess water, then lay wrapper flat on clean counter.

WRAPPING UP REFRESHMENT

In tropical Vietnam, where summers are hot and humid, gỏi cuốn make for a refreshing light meal or appetizer. Translated as "summer rolls" or "salad rolls," they're made with crisp vegetables, springy rice noodles, lots of fragrant herbs, and morsels of protein (fish, shrimp, and pork are common), all wrapped up in a translucent rice paper wrapper. These wrappers, called bánh tráng, are made from a mixture of rice, water, and salt that has been spread into an ultrathin crepe, steamed, and then dried until hard. To cook with them, you need to quickly rehydrate them in water until they're soft and pliable.

HOW TO ASSEMBLE A SUMMER ROLL

Traditional recipes for gỏi cuốn layer sliced shrimp throughout the rolls, but we found that keeping the shrimp whole eliminated some tricky knife work and made the rolls easier to shape. Forming these rolls takes practice! If your first couple rolls don't turn out that well, don't worry—just chop them up and eat them like a salad, they'll still taste delicious. The hydrated rice paper wrappers are quite sticky, so make sure that your shaped rolls don't touch one other, or they'll stick together!

1. Fold 1 lettuce leaf in half and place on lower third of wrapper, leaving about ½-inch border on each side. Spread ⅓ cup noodles on top of lettuce, then sprinkle with 1 teaspoon scallions. Spread ¼ cup herb mixture on top.

2. Bring lower edge of wrapper up and over herbs.

3. Roll snugly but gently until greens and noodles are enclosed.

4. Fold in sides of wrapper to enclose ends.

5. Arrange 3 shrimp on top of remaining wrapper.

6. Continue to roll until filling is completely enclosed in wrapper, forming neat cylinder.

NAAN FLATBREAD

with Spiced-Yogurt Paneer

BEFORE YOU BEGIN

▶ You can substitute ¼ cup cooked, shredded chicken or drained, rinsed chickpeas for the paneer.

▶ Try dolloping your baked flatbread with mango chutney or drizzling it with date-tamarind sauce.

"It was gone within minutes."
—Crystal, 14

PREPARE INGREDIENTS

YOGURT MARINADE

- 1 small garlic clove, peeled and minced (see page 13)
- ¾ teaspoon garam masala
- ¼ teaspoon ground cumin
- ⅛ teaspoon ground ginger
- ⅛ teaspoon salt
- ⅛ teaspoon pepper
- 1 teaspoon extra-virgin olive oil
- 2 tablespoons plain whole-milk yogurt
- 1 teaspoon lime juice, squeezed from ½ lime
- 1 ounce paneer, cut into ½-inch cubes (¼ cup)

FLATBREAD

- 1 teaspoon extra-virgin olive oil
- 1 (8-inch) naan
- ⅓ cup shredded mozzarella cheese (1½ ounces)
- 1 tablespoon finely chopped red onion (see page 13)
- 1 teaspoon chopped fresh cilantro (see page 13)

START COOKING!

1. For the yogurt marinade: Adjust oven rack to lowest position and heat oven to 400 degrees. In small microwave-safe bowl, use spoon to stir together garlic, garam masala, cumin, ginger, salt, pepper, and 1 teaspoon oil. Microwave until fragrant, about 15 seconds.

2. Add yogurt and lime juice to bowl with garlic mixture and stir until well combined. Add paneer and stir until coated.

3. For the flatbread: Use pastry brush to brush 1 teaspoon oil into 9-inch circle in center of rimmed baking sheet. Place naan on top of oil.

4. Sprinkle mozzarella over naan, leaving ½-inch border around edge. Spoon paneer on top (some marinade will be left behind in bowl). Sprinkle evenly with onion.

5. Bake until naan is golden brown around edges and mozzarella is bubbling, 10 to 12 minutes.

6. Use oven mitts to transfer baking sheet to cooling rack. Let cool slightly, about 2 minutes. Use spatula to transfer naan to cutting board. Sprinkle with cilantro. Use chef's knife to cut naan into wedges. Serve.

A FABULOUS FLATBREAD

This delicious concoction is kind of like a pizza and kind of like a flatbread, all rolled up in Indian-inspired flavors and baked to perfection. We topped chewy naan with melty mozzarella cheese, sprinkles of red onion and fresh cilantro, plus tender cubes of paneer coated in a tangy, spiced (but not spicy!) yogurt marinade. The result? A flatbread you'll want all to yourself.

GETTING TO KNOW GRAINS

▶ Grains, from chewy farro to tender white rice, can be a simple side dish, an ideal base for Crispy Tofu Bowls with Vegetables (see page 92) or Spicy Burrito Bowls (see page 96), or a star ingredient in Vegetable Stir-Fried Rice (see page 138). Lots of grains are easy to cook using the pasta method (in lots of boiling water, just like with pasta). You can save time by cooking your grains ahead of time; they'll just need a quick zap in the microwave before you start cooking—or eating.

HOW TO COOK GRAINS USING THE PASTA METHOD

In large pot, bring **water** to boil. Add **grains** and **salt**, following measurements below. Use wooden spoon to stir to combine. Cook until tender, following timing below. Drain grains well in colander. Grains can be cooked, cooled, and refrigerated in airtight container for up to 3 days. If serving immediately, season with **salt** and **pepper** to taste (see page 15).

HOW TO REHEAT GRAINS

To reheat grains, microwave in covered microwave-safe bowl until hot throughout, fluffing with fork halfway through cooking (timing will vary depending on the quantity and type of grains used). Season with **salt** and **pepper** to taste (see page 15).

GRAIN	DRY AMOUNT (CUPS)	WATER (QUARTS)	SALT (TEASPOONS)	COOKED YIELD (CUPS)	COOKING TIME (MINUTES)
Pearl barley	¾	2	½	2	20 to 40
	1½	4	1	4	
Farro	¾	2	½	2	15 to 30
	1½	4	1	4	
Black rice	¾	2	½	2	20 to 25
	1½	4	1	4	
Long-grain brown rice	¾	2	½	2	25 to 30
	1½	4	1	4	
Long-grain white rice	¾	2	½	2	10 to 15
	1½	4	1	4	
Short-grain brown rice	¾	2	½	2	30 to 35
	1½	4	1	4	
Wild rice	¾	2	½	2	35 to 40
	1½	4	1	4	
Oat berries	¾	2	½	1½	30 to 40
	1½	4	1	3	
Wheat berries	¾	4	1	1½	60 to 70
	1½	4	1	3	

CRISPY TOFU BOWLS

with Vegetables

BEFORE YOU BEGIN

▶ Make the short-grain brown rice (or other grain of your choice, see page 90) before you start the recipe.

▶ You can substitute extra-firm tofu for the firm tofu, if desired. Do not use soft or silken tofu for this recipe.

"This was the first time I've made tofu and I gotta say, it was great!"
—Anna, 16

PREPARE INGREDIENTS

BOWL

- 2 cups cooked short-grain brown rice or other grain of your choice, warmed up (see page 90)

- 7 ounces firm tofu, cut into 3-by-¾-inch sticks (see photos, below right)

- ⅛ teaspoon salt

- ⅛ teaspoon pepper

- 3 tablespoons cornstarch

- 1 tablespoon vegetable oil

- 3 radishes, sliced thin

- ½ cucumber, halved lengthwise, seeded, and sliced thin

- ½ ripe avocado, pitted and cut into ½-inch pieces (see page 14)

- 1 (8-by-7½-inch) sheet nori, crumbled (optional)

DRESSING

- 2 tablespoons soy sauce

- 1 tablespoon unseasoned rice vinegar

- 1 tablespoon mirin

- ¼ teaspoon grated lime zest plus 1 tablespoon juice, zested and squeezed from ½ lime

- 1 scallion, root end trimmed, white part minced, green part sliced thin

- ½ teaspoon grated fresh ginger (see page 94)

- ¼ teaspoon toasted sesame oil

START COOKING!

1. For the bowl: Line large plate with paper towels. Spread tofu over paper towel–lined plate and let drain for 20 minutes.

2. For the dressing: While tofu drains, in small bowl, whisk together all dressing ingredients until well combined.

3. When tofu is ready, gently pat dry with paper towels. Sprinkle drained tofu with salt and pepper. Place cornstarch in shallow dish. Gently toss tofu with cornstarch until coated. Line plate with fresh paper towels.

keep going >>>

HOW TO CUT TOFU

1. Place block of tofu on cutting board. Use chef's knife to slice block of tofu crosswise (the short way) into ¾-inch slabs.

2. Then use chef's knife to slice each slab into ¾-inch-thick sticks.

4. In 10-inch nonstick skillet, heat vegetable oil over medium-high heat until shimmering, about 2 minutes (oil should be hot but not smoking). Add tofu and cook until lightly browned on all sides, 12 to 15 minutes, using tongs to turn tofu every few minutes. Turn off heat. Transfer tofu to paper towel–lined plate to drain.

5. In medium bowl, combine warm, cooked rice and half of dressing. Use rubber spatula to toss to combine. Season with salt and pepper to taste (see page 15).

6. Divide rice evenly between 2 serving bowls. Top each bowl with crispy tofu, radishes, cucumber, and avocado. Drizzle remaining dressing evenly over each bowl, and sprinkle with nori (if using). Serve.

FOR CRISPY TOFU, USE A CORNSTARCH COATING

One of the best parts of this bowl is the supercrispy tofu. (If you're a tofu newbie, this recipe's for you!) That texture is all thanks to the tofu's cornstarch coating. When cornstarch comes in contact with moist tofu, the starch absorbs some of the tofu's water. When the wet cornstarch heats up, the starch molecules spread out to become a tangled network that traps tiny pockets of water. When it gets hot enough, the water evaporates as steam, leaving behind a rigid, crackly network of starch molecules that's perfectly—you guessed it—crispy.

HOW TO PEEL, GRATE, AND SLICE GINGER

To peel: Place ginger on cutting board and hold firmly with one hand. Use vegetable peeler to peel off brown outer layer of ginger, peeling away from you.

To grate: Rub peeled ginger back and forth against surface of rasp grater.

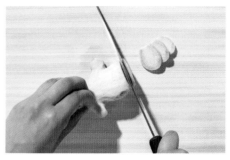

To slice: Use chef's knife to thinly slice peeled ginger crosswise (the short way).

ANATOMY OF A GREAT GRAIN BOWL

▶ There aren't a whole lot of rules when it comes to building a great grain bowl, but there are a few elements that will take your bowls from boring to brilliant. Start with one of the recipes in this chapter, or create your own fully customized version.

BASE

Filling grains (see page 90) make a great bowl base. Tossing your grains with some sauce or dressing adds flavor to each and every bite.

SAUCE

Great bowls use sauces or dressings to amp up their flavor and moisture—both homemade and store-bought varieties are excellent options.

PROTEIN

The beauty of bowls is that they're flexible—you can add protein in the form of cooked chopped, ground, or shredded meat; eggs; beans; or tofu.

CRUNCH

Adding some crunch takes a bowl from good to great. Tortilla chips take our Spicy Burrito Bowls (see page 96) over the top, while our Crispy Tofu Bowls (see page 92) have crunchy radishes and cucumbers. Raid your pantry or fridge for even more crunchy goodness.

BEGINNER

VEGETARIAN

SERVES 2 / 35 MINUTES
plus time to make
rice and Pickled
Red Onions

SPICY BURRITO BOWLS

BEFORE YOU BEGIN

▶ Make the long-grain white rice (or grain of your choice, see page 90) and Pickled Red Onions (see right) before you start the recipe.

▶ Top your burrito bowl with shredded cheese, sour cream, or salsa.

"This recipe is really tasty and fast to make! So much better than fast food."
—Adam, 17

PREPARE INGREDIENTS

- 2 cups cooked long-grain white rice or other grain of your choice, warmed up (see page 90)

- 1 recipe Pickled Red Onions (see below right)

- 1 tablespoon plus 2 teaspoons extra-virgin olive oil, measured separately

- ½ small onion, peeled and finely chopped (see page 13)

- ¼ teaspoon salt

- 2 garlic cloves, peeled and minced (see page 13)

- 1 teaspoon chili powder

- 1 teaspoon minced canned chipotle chile in adobo sauce

- 1 teaspoon ground cumin

- 1 (15-ounce) can pinto beans, drained and rinsed

- 1 cup canned tomato sauce

- ¼ cup water

- 2 teaspoons lime juice, squeezed from 1 lime, plus lime wedges for serving

- 2 tablespoons chopped fresh cilantro, plus extra for serving (see page 13)

- 1 ripe avocado, halved, pitted, and cut into ½-inch pieces (see page 14)

- 1 cup (1 ounce) tortilla chips

START COOKING!

1. In 10-inch nonstick skillet, heat 1 tablespoon oil over medium heat until shimmering, about 2 minutes (oil should be hot but not smoking). Add finely chopped onion and salt and cook, using rubber spatula to stir occasionally, until softened, about 5 minutes.

2. Stir in garlic, chili powder, chipotle, and cumin and cook until fragrant, about 30 seconds.

3. Add pinto beans, tomato sauce, and water and bring to simmer (small bubbles should break often across surface of mixture). Reduce heat to low and cook, stirring occasionally, until mixture is slightly thickened, about 3 minutes. Turn off heat.

4. In medium bowl, whisk together lime juice, cilantro, and remaining 2 teaspoons oil. Add warm, cooked rice and stir until well combined. Season with salt and pepper to taste (see page 15).

5. Divide rice evenly between 2 serving bowls. Top each bowl with beans, avocado, tortilla chips, pickled red onions, and extra cilantro. Serve with lime wedges.

PICKLED RED ONIONS

- 1 small red onion

- 1 cup white wine vinegar

- 2 tablespoons lime juice, squeezed from 1 lime

- 1 tablespoon sugar

- 1 teaspoon salt

Place onion on cutting board and use chef's knife to slice into thin strips (see page 13). Place sliced onion in medium bowl. In small saucepan, combine vinegar, lime juice, sugar, and salt. Bring to boil over high heat. Turn off heat. Pour vinegar mixture over onions. Let mixture cool completely, about 30 minutes. Drain onions in fine-mesh strainer, discarding liquid. (Pickled onions can be refrigerated for up to 4 days.)

SHIITAKE-BEEF RAMEN

BEFORE YOU BEGIN

▶ You can substitute an equal amount of cremini or white mushrooms for the shiitake mushrooms.

"I used to make ramen all the time just plain. Now I know what to do to make it a good meal."
—Brody, 14

PREPARE INGREDIENTS

- 4 ounces sirloin steak tips, trimmed and cut into 2-inch pieces
- ⅛ teaspoon salt
- ⅛ teaspoon pepper
- 1 tablespoon vegetable oil
- 4 ounces shiitake mushrooms, stemmed and sliced thin
- 3 scallions, root ends trimmed and scallions sliced into 1-inch pieces
- 1 tablespoon toasted sesame oil
- 1 tablespoon white miso
- 2 teaspoons grated fresh ginger (see page 94)
- 3 cups chicken broth
- 1 cup water
- 2 packages ramen noodles, seasoning packets discarded
- 1 cup (1 ounce) baby spinach
- 2 teaspoons soy sauce

   Toppings (see Up Your Game, below right)

STRENGTH IN NOODLES

Chewy, springy ramen noodles are originally from China and are made with wheat flour, salt, water, and an alkaline solution called kansui. (Alkalinity is the opposite of acidity.) Kansui literally changes the chemistry of the flour, increasing the amount of gluten it forms and creating firmer, bouncier noodles. Unlike Italian pasta, which gets mushy when it hangs out in a big bowl of soup for too long, alkaline ramen noodles hold onto their texture until your very last bite.

START COOKING!

1. Pat steak dry with paper towels and sprinkle with salt and pepper.

2. In large saucepan, heat vegetable oil over medium heat until shimmering, about 2 minutes (oil should be hot but not smoking). Add steak and cook, using tongs to flip, until well browned all over and meat registers 120 to 125 degrees on instant-read thermometer (for medium-rare; see page 10), 4 to 6 minutes.

3. Transfer steak to cutting board, cover loosely with aluminum foil, and let rest until ready to serve.

4. Add mushrooms and scallions to now-empty saucepan. Cook, using wooden spoon to stir occasionally, until vegetables are browned and tender, about 3 minutes.

5. Stir in sesame oil, miso, and ginger and cook, stirring constantly, until fragrant, about 30 seconds. Stir in broth and water, scraping up browned bits on bottom of saucepan, and bring to boil.

6. Add noodles and cook, stirring occasionally to break up noodles, until tender, about 3 minutes. Turn off heat and slide saucepan to cool burner. Stir in spinach and soy sauce. Ladle soup into 2 serving bowls.

7. Use chef's knife to slice steak thin against grain (see photo, page 118). Divide steak evenly between bowls of soup. Add your favorite toppings. Serve.

▶ ▶ ▶ UP YOUR GAME

Get creative and make your ramen your own by adding different toppings, such as **corn**, thinly sliced **scallions**, **bean sprouts**, shredded **nori**, a **Jammy Egg** (see page 37), **sriracha sauce**, **chili crisp**, **chile-garlic sauce**, and/or **kimchi**.

CHICKEN TORTILLA SOUP

BEFORE YOU BEGIN

▶ You can substitute two (5- to 7-ounce) bone-in chicken thighs for the chicken breast.

▶ Top your soup with diced avocado, shredded cheese, minced jalapeño, and/or Mexican crema, if desired.

"Even though I'm really picky, I tried it and really liked it."
—Skyler, 15

PREPARE INGREDIENTS

TORTILLA STRIPS

4   (6-inch) corn tortillas, cut into ½-inch strips

1   teaspoon vegetable oil

⅛   teaspoon salt

SOUP

1   small onion, peeled and cut into quarters

1   tomato, cored (see page 155) and cut into quarters

2   garlic cloves, peeled

1–2   teaspoons minced canned chipotle chile in adobo sauce

2   teaspoons vegetable oil

⅛   teaspoon salt

1   (12-ounce) bone-in split chicken breast, skin removed

4   cups chicken broth

2   tablespoons fresh cilantro leaves

Lime wedges for serving

TURNING UP THE FLAVOR IN TORTILLA SOUP

Our tortilla soup starts with a sofrito—a sautéed blend of aromatic vegetables, including smoky chipotle chiles in adobo sauce, that forms its flavor base. Cooking the chicken breast directly in the soup lets the chicken absorb all those flavors while also giving the broth an extra chicken-y boost.

START COOKING!

1. For the tortilla strips: Adjust oven rack to middle position and heat oven to 425 degrees. Place tortilla strips on rimmed baking sheet, drizzle with 1 teaspoon oil, and toss to coat evenly. Spread tortilla strips in single layer.

2. Bake tortilla strips until deep golden brown and crispy, 7 to 10 minutes, using oven mitts to rotate baking sheet halfway through baking (see page 15). Transfer baking sheet to cooling rack. Sprinkle tortilla strips with ⅛ teaspoon salt and let cool while making soup.

3. For the soup: Add onion, tomato, garlic, and chipotle to food processor. Lock lid into place. Process mixture until smooth, about 30 seconds. Remove lid and carefully remove processor blade.

4. In large saucepan, add tomato mixture, 2 teaspoons oil, and ⅛ teaspoon salt. Cook over medium-high heat, stirring occasionally with rubber spatula, until tomato mixture has reduced and thickened, about 8 minutes.

5. Add chicken and broth to tomato mixture and bring to boil. Reduce heat to low and cover pot with lid. Cook until chicken registers 160 degrees on instant-read thermometer (see page 10), about 20 minutes.

6. Use tongs to transfer chicken to cutting board and let chicken cool slightly, about 5 minutes (continue to cook soup over low heat while chicken cools). Use 2 forks to shred chicken into bite-size pieces.

7. Add shredded chicken back to soup and cook until heated through, about 2 minutes. Turn off heat.

8. Divide tortilla strips evenly between 2 serving bowls. Ladle soup into bowls and sprinkle with cilantro. Serve with lime wedges.

SPICE-RUBBED ROAST CHICKEN

BEFORE YOU BEGIN

▶ Giblets are a bundle of small organs that are sometimes found in a packet inside the cavity of the chicken. Check for them and if they're there, discard them before putting the chicken in the oven—you won't need them.

"It was crisp, juicy, and full of flavor!"
—Claudio, 14

PREPARE INGREDIENTS

- 1 tablespoon chili powder
- 1 tablespoon dried oregano
- 2 teaspoons kosher salt
- 1 teaspoon garlic powder or granulated garlic
- 1 teaspoon pepper
- 1 (3½- to 4-pound) whole chicken, giblets discarded
- 1 tablespoon plus 1 tablespoon extra-virgin olive oil, measured separately
- ½ cup water
- 1 teaspoon cornstarch
- 2 teaspoons lemon juice, squeezed from 1 lemon

START COOKING!

1. Adjust oven rack to middle position and heat oven to 400 degrees. In small bowl, use spoon to stir together chili powder, oregano, salt, garlic powder, and pepper.

2. Transfer chicken, breast side down, to 12-inch ovensafe skillet. Use paper towels to pat chicken dry on all sides. Use your hands to rub exposed side with 1 tablespoon oil. Sprinkle with half of spice mixture.

3. Flip chicken breast side up. Rub exposed side with remaining 1 tablespoon oil and sprinkle with remaining spice mixture. Wash your hands.

4. Transfer skillet to oven and roast until breast registers 160 degrees and drumsticks and thighs register 175 degrees on instant-read thermometer (see page 106), 50 minutes to 1 hour.

keep going >>>

▶ ▶ ▶ *UP YOUR GAME*

You can change up the flavor of your roast chicken by using other combinations of spices and dried herbs. Experiment with what you have in your spice cabinet, or try one of these flavor profiles.

Spice-Rubbed Roast Chicken with Dill and Garlic: Omit chili powder and oregano. Add 1 tablespoon **dried dill** to bowl along with other seasonings in step 1.

Spice-Rubbed Roast Chicken with Coriander and Lemon: Omit chili powder and oregano. Add 1 tablespoon **ground coriander** and 1 tablespoon **grated lemon zest** to bowl along with other seasonings in step 1.

5. Use oven mitts to remove skillet from oven and place on cooling rack. Place oven mitt on skillet handle as reminder that handle is HOT. Insert wooden spoon into chicken cavity, hold outside of chicken with tongs, and transfer chicken to carving board. Let chicken rest for 20 minutes. (Do not discard drippings in pan.)

6. While chicken rests, in second small bowl, use clean spoon to stir water and cornstarch until dissolved.

7. Holding skillet handle with oven mitt, add cornstarch mixture to drippings in skillet and place over medium-high heat. Whisk to scrape up any browned bits from bottom of pan. Cook until mixture is boiling and slightly thickened, about 2 minutes. Turn off heat and slide skillet to cool burner. Whisk in lemon juice.

8. Use chef's knife to carve chicken, following photos, far right. Serve, passing sauce separately.

GIVE IT A REST

You just pulled this golden-brown roast chicken out of the oven and you're dying to dig in—we get it. But trust us, it's worth the 20-minute wait to make sure that your chicken is as juicy as possible. Why? As chicken cooks, its muscle fibers contract, squeezing out liquid. Letting the chicken rest for a bit once it's out of the oven allows those fibers to loosen up and draw that moisture back into the meat. If you carved your chicken right away, all of those juices would end up on your cutting board instead of in your chicken. And not to worry—after its 20-minute rest your chicken will still be piping hot.

HOW TO TEMP A WHOLE CHICKEN

The best way to tell when chicken is fully cooked is to measure its temperature with an instant-read thermometer. As you temp, make sure to keep the thermometer away from any bones—they can give you inaccurate readings.

To temp breast: Insert instant-read thermometer into thickest part of chicken breast, holding it parallel to bird, avoiding bone. Breast should register 160 degrees.

To temp thigh: Insert instant-read thermometer at angle into area between drumstick and breast, avoiding bone. Thigh should register 175 degrees.

HOW TO CARVE A CHICKEN

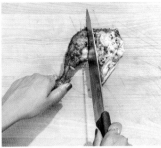

1. Cut chicken where leg meets breast, holding knife close to leg quarter to keep plenty of skin covering breast. Pull leg quarter away from breast while pushing up on joint. Cut through joint and skin to remove leg quarter.

2. Place leg quarter skin side down on carving board. Cut through joint that connects drumstick to thigh. Repeat steps 1 and 2 on second leg quarter.

3. With cavity facing away from you, locate breastbone. Starting at cavity end of breast, cut just off center of breastbone. Working from cavity end to neck end and using breastbone as guide, cut straight down along breastbone until you reach rib cage.

4. Insert your thumb into cut. Gently pull back breast to expose rib cage. Working from cavity end to neck end, cut breast from rib cage. As you cut, angle knife to follow curve of rib cage.

5. Continue to cut until you reach wing joint. Gently pull breast away from rib cage while pushing up on wing joint from underneath. Cut through wing joint to remove breast and wing.

6. Placing knife as close to wing bone as possible, cut wing from breast by slicing through skin and connective tissue. Slice breast crosswise (the short way). Repeat steps 3 through 6 on second breast.

ARROZ CON POLLO

(Chicken and Rice)

BEFORE YOU BEGIN

▶ Sazón is a spice blend common in Latin American cooking. Look for it in the Latin section of your grocery store or in Latin markets.

▶ You can substitute long-grain rice for medium-grain, but the rice will be slightly less creamy.

PREPARE INGREDIENTS

CHICKEN

- 1 tablespoon distilled white vinegar
- ¾ teaspoon pepper
- ¼ teaspoon dried oregano
- ½ teaspoon salt
- 1½ pounds boneless skinless chicken thighs

SOFRITO

- 1 tomato, cored (see page 155) and chopped
- 1 green bell pepper, stemmed, seeded, and chopped
- ½ onion, peeled and chopped (see page 13)
- ¾ cup chopped fresh cilantro leaves and stems (see page 13)
- 6 garlic cloves, peeled
- ¾ teaspoon ground cumin

RICE

- 1½ cups medium-grain rice
- 1 tablespoon extra-virgin olive oil
- ½ onion, peeled and chopped (see page 13)
- 1 tablespoon sazón seasoning (store-bought, or see page 110)
- 1¼ cups chicken broth
- ¼ cup sliced green olives with pimento
- 1 bay leaf
- 1 teaspoon salt
- ½ cup frozen peas, thawed (optional)

START COOKING!

1. Adjust oven rack to middle position and heat oven to 350 degrees.

2. For the chicken: In large bowl, combine vinegar, pepper, oregano, and ½ teaspoon salt. Add chicken and use rubber spatula to toss until chicken is well coated. Let sit on counter while making sofrito.

3. For the sofrito: Meanwhile, add all sofrito ingredients to food processor and lock lid into place. Process until vegetables are pureed, about 20 seconds, scraping down bowl with clean rubber spatula as needed. Remove lid and carefully remove processor blade.

keep going >>>

A ONE-POT CARIBBEAN CLASSIC

Families across Latin America have their own versions of arroz con pollo, featuring many different ingredients and flavors. In this recipe, we nod to Puerto Rican and Cuban versions through ingredients such as flavor-packed sazón seasoning, briny green olives, and a sofrito.

To streamline our recipe, we start with boneless, skinless chicken thighs—they're small enough to nestle and cook in the brothy rice mixture and they're easy to shred right in the pot (no bones to get in the way!). A simple marinade seasons the chicken inside and out and gives it a punch of tangy flavor from the vinegar. Cooking the rice and chicken in a covered pot in the oven exposes it to heat on all sides so that both of our star ingredients cook quickly and evenly.

4. For the rice: Set fine-mesh strainer over large bowl and set in sink. Place rice in strainer and rinse under cold running water, emptying bowl a few times as it fills, until water in bowl is clear, 1½ to 2 minutes. Shake strainer to drain rice well and set aside. Discard water in bowl.

5. Heat oil in Dutch oven over medium heat until shimmering, about 2 minutes (oil should be hot but not smoking). Add remaining ½ onion and cook, stirring occasionally, until softened, about 5 minutes.

6. Add rice and sazón and cook, stirring often, for 2 minutes. Stir in sofrito, broth, olives, bay leaf, and 1 teaspoon salt.

7. Add chicken to pot and nestle chicken into rice, making sure chicken is covered in liquid (see photo, below right). Increase heat to high and bring mixture to boil, then immediately turn off heat. Cover pot with lid.

8. Use oven mitts to transfer pot to oven and bake for 30 minutes. Transfer pot to cooling rack and let sit, covered, for 15 minutes.

9. Carefully remove lid and discard bay leaf (be careful, pot will still be VERY HOT). Use 2 forks to shred chicken in pot. Fluff rice with fork and gently stir in peas (if using). Let sit for 2 minutes while peas warm through. Serve.

DIY SAZÓN SEASONING

If you can't find sazón seasoning at your grocery store, it's easy to make at home. In our blend, we use paprika to mimic the orange-red color of ground annatto seeds typically used in sazón. This recipe yields 1 tablespoon, just the right amount for one batch of our Arroz con Pollo.

    1   teaspoon garlic powder

    ¾   teaspoon salt

    ½   teaspoon paprika

    ½   teaspoon ground coriander

    ¼   teaspoon ground cumin

In small bowl, use spoon to stir all sazón ingredients until well combined.

HOW TO NESTLE CHICKEN INTO RICE

Use tongs to add chicken to pot and nestle chicken into rice, making sure chicken is covered in liquid.

BUTTERMILK FRIED CHICKEN

BEFORE YOU BEGIN

▶ You will need a large Dutch oven that holds 6 quarts or more for this recipe.

▶ For more information on how to fry safely and how to handle frying oil, see page 11.

"I enjoyed the crispiness of the chicken."
—Amber, 17

PREPARE INGREDIENTS

2 cups buttermilk

1 tablespoon plus ½ teaspoon salt, measured separately

3 pounds bone-in chicken pieces (split breasts cut in half crosswise, drumsticks, and/or thighs)

2 cups all-purpose flour

1 tablespoon pepper

1 tablespoon dried oregano

1 tablespoon garlic powder

1 tablespoon onion powder

1 teaspoon cayenne pepper (optional)

6–7 cups peanut or vegetable oil for frying

START COOKING!

1. In large bowl, whisk buttermilk and 1 tablespoon salt until salt is dissolved. Add chicken to bowl, cover with plastic wrap, and refrigerate for at least 30 minutes and up to 24 hours.

2. Meanwhile, clean and dry whisk. In second large bowl, whisk together flour, pepper, oregano, garlic powder, onion powder, cayenne pepper (if using), and remaining ½ teaspoon salt.

3. Place cooling rack inside rimmed baking sheet and set aside.

4. When chicken is ready, remove bowl from refrigerator and discard plastic wrap.

keep going >>>

HOW TO TEMP FRIED CHICKEN

Use tongs to carefully transfer chicken to paper towel–lined cooling rack. Use instant-read thermometer to measure temperature of chicken (use tongs to return chicken to oil to continue cooking, if necessary).

SECRETS TO THE ULTIMATE FRIED CHICKEN

Juicy, crispy fried chicken can be yours—if you follow these two key techniques.

Rise and Brine: As the chicken sits in the brine—the mixture of buttermilk and salt—some of the salt and some of the water in the buttermilk make their way into the chicken, seasoning it inside and out. The salt also changes the structure of the chicken's proteins, helping it hold onto that extra water, even after it's cooked. Bonus: Acidic buttermilk helps to create even more tender chicken. The result: juicy, perfectly seasoned chicken.

Put a Lid on It: When you add cold chicken to hot frying oil, the oil's temperature drops dramatically. Covering the Dutch oven for the first half of cooking helps the oil reheat quickly—and hotter oil creates that iconic crispy, crunchy fried chicken coating.

5. Working with 1 piece of chicken at a time, dredge chicken in flour mixture following photos, right. Repeat with remaining chicken. Discard flour mixture and buttermilk brine. Wash your hands.

6. Add oil to large Dutch oven until it measures 1 inch deep. Heat oil over medium-high heat until it registers 350 degrees on instant-read thermometer.

7. Use tongs to carefully place chicken in oil, skin side down, in single layer (some slight overlap is OK).

8. Place lid on Dutch oven and cook for 10 minutes. (As the chicken cooks, you will see a lot of steam coming out from under the lid—this is OK!)

9. Meanwhile, wash and dry cooling rack and baking sheet. Place clean cooling rack in clean baking sheet and line cooling rack with triple layer of paper towels. Place on counter next to stovetop.

10. Use oven mitts to quickly remove lid (lid will be very hot; be careful not to drip condensation into oil). Use clean tongs to carefully flip chicken.

11. Cook chicken, uncovered, until deep golden brown and breasts register 160 degrees and thighs/drumsticks register 175 degrees on instant-read thermometer (see page 113), 6 to 10 minutes. (As chicken cooks, check temperature of oil and adjust stove's heat as needed so that oil stays at 275 degrees.)

12. Transfer chicken to paper towel–lined rack as each piece finishes cooking. Turn off heat and cover Dutch oven with lid. Let oil cool completely (see page 11). Let chicken rest for 10 minutes. Serve.

HOW TO DREDGE CHICKEN

1. Working with 1 piece of chicken at a time, remove chicken from bowl with brine and shake off excess buttermilk.

2. Place piece of chicken in bowl with flour mixture. Turn chicken and press to coat chicken on all sides. Shake off excess flour and transfer chicken to cooling rack set in rimmed baking sheet. Repeat with remaining chicken.

STEAK TACOS
with Charred Corn Salsa

BEFORE YOU BEGIN

▶ Serve these tacos with your favorite toppings, such as sour cream, chopped avocado, sliced radishes, crumbled queso fresco, hot sauce, and/or extra chopped cilantro.

"My older brother ate four and said it was a 12/10! He wants the recipe to take with him to college."
—Acacia, 15

PREPARE INGREDIENTS

1   small red onion, peeled, ¼ of onion finely chopped and ¾ of onion sliced thin (see page 13)

1   jalapeño chile, stemmed, seeded, and minced (see page 14)

2   tablespoons lime juice, squeezed from 1 lime

2   tablespoons chopped fresh cilantro (see page 13)

¾   teaspoon plus 1 teaspoon salt, measured separately

½   teaspoon plus ½ teaspoon pepper, measured separately

1   tablespoon ground cumin

1   (1½-pound) flank steak

1   tablespoon plus 1 teaspoon vegetable oil, measured separately

1   large poblano chile, stemmed, seeded, halved crosswise, and sliced thin

1½ cups frozen corn, thawed

10–12 (6-inch) corn tortillas

START COOKING!

1. In medium bowl, combine chopped onion, jalapeño, lime juice, cilantro, ¾ teaspoon salt, and ½ teaspoon pepper; set aside.

2. In small bowl, use spoon to stir together cumin, remaining 1 teaspoon salt, and remaining ½ teaspoon pepper.

3. Place steak on cutting board and use chef's knife to cut steak lengthwise (the long way; with the grain) into 3 equal pieces (see photo, page 118). Use paper towels to pat both sides of steaks dry. Sprinkle steaks evenly with half of cumin mixture. Flip steaks and sprinkle evenly with remaining cumin mixture. Wash your hands.

4. In 12-inch skillet, heat 1 tablespoon oil over medium-high heat until just beginning to smoke, about 3 minutes. (You should start to see wisps of smoke coming up from oil; you may need to get eye level with skillet to see this. Turn on your stove's vent hood, if you have one.)

keep going >>>

ONE PAN, THREE STAGES

To bring the charred flavor of grilled steak tacos indoors we turned to our trusty 12-inch skillet. This kitchen workhorse does triple duty in this recipe: First, we use it to sear our steaks until they have a beautifully browned crust and a juicy pink interior. While our steaks rest, our skillet tackles its next task: cooking sliced onion and poblano chile. As the vegetables cook, they pick up the savory browned bits left behind by the beef. Finally, we crank up the heat for stage three: making a charred corn salsa. The skillet's heat browns the outside of the corn kernels, giving our salsa a hit of smoky-sweet flavor. Pile your tortillas with steak, vegetables, and salsa and get ready to meet your new favorite dinner.

5. Use tongs to carefully lay steaks in skillet, spaced slightly apart. Cook, without moving, until browned on first side, about 3 minutes. Flip steaks and cook until browned on second side, about 3 minutes. While steaks cook, wash and dry cutting board.

6. Flip steaks and cook, flipping as needed to ensure even browning, until well browned and meat registers 120 to 125 degrees on instant-read thermometer for medium-rare (see page 10), 2 to 4 minutes longer.

7. Use tongs to transfer steaks to clean cutting board. Let steaks rest while cooking vegetables.

8. Reduce heat to medium. Add poblano and sliced onion to now-empty skillet and cook, stirring occasionally with wooden spoon and scraping up browned bits on bottom of skillet, until peppers are softened and onions are well browned, 8 to 10 minutes. Transfer vegetables to second small bowl.

9. Increase heat to high. Add corn and remaining 1 teaspoon oil to now-empty skillet. Cover with lid and cook until lightly charred and kernels begin to pop, 3 to 5 minutes, shaking skillet halfway through cooking. Turn off heat. Transfer corn to bowl with onion-jalapeño mixture and stir until combined.

10. Stack tortillas on small microwave-safe plate; cover with damp dish towel; and microwave until warm, 30 seconds to 1 minute.

11. Use clean chef's knife to slice steak thin crosswise (the short way; against grain, see photo, right). Serve with warm tortillas, poblano mixture, and corn salsa.

HOW TO CUT RAW FLANK STEAK

Place steak on cutting board and use chef's knife to cut steak lengthwise (the long way; with the grain) into 3 equal pieces.

HOW TO SLICE COOKED FLANK STEAK

Use clean chef's knife to slice steak thin crosswise (the short way; against the grain).

CHEESEBURGER SLIDERS

BEFORE YOU BEGIN

▶ This recipe moves quickly, so be sure to have all your ingredients prepared before you begin cooking. If you have a kitchen scale, use it to weigh the beef into equal 2-ounce portions in step 5.

"Great to make for friends."
—Evan, 17

PREPARE INGREDIENTS

BURGER SAUCE

- ¼ cup mayonnaise
- 2 tablespoons ketchup
- 1 teaspoon sweet pickle relish
- 1 teaspoon sugar
- 1 teaspoon distilled white vinegar

SLIDERS

- 12 (2½-inch) slider buns or soft dinner rolls, halved horizontally
- 6 slices deli American cheese
- 1½ pounds 85 percent lean ground beef
- 1½ teaspoons kosher salt
- 1 teaspoon pepper
- 1 teaspoon plus 1 teaspoon vegetable oil, measured separately
- ¼ cup plus ¼ cup finely chopped onion, measured separately (see page 13)
- 2 tablespoons plus 2 tablespoons water, measured separately

START COOKING!

1. For the burger sauce: In medium bowl, whisk together all burger sauce ingredients.

2. For the sliders: Separate bun bottoms from bun tops. Place bun bottoms on serving platter. Use 1-teaspoon measuring spoon to spread 1 heaping teaspoon burger sauce onto each bun bottom. Set aside bun bottoms.

3. Stack slices of cheese on cutting board. Use chef's knife to cut into quarters (you will have 24 pieces). Separate cheese into 12 stacks with 2 pieces in each stack. Set aside with bun tops.

4. Use scissors to cut open seams along sides of quart-size zipper-lock plastic bag, but leave bottom seam intact.

5. Divide beef into 12 equal portions (2 ounces each) and place on rimmed baking sheet. Use your hands to roll each portion into ball. Wash your hands.

6. Place 1 ball in zipper-lock bag and fold top of bag over ball. Use clear pie plate on top of plastic to press ball into even 4-inch circle, about ¼ inch thick (see photo, page 122). Remove patty from zipper-lock bag and return it to baking sheet. Repeat with remaining balls. Sprinkle patties evenly with salt and pepper. Wash your hands.

keep going >>>

7. Heat 1 teaspoon oil in 12-inch nonstick skillet over medium-high heat until just beginning to smoke, about 3 minutes. (You should start to see wisps of smoke coming up from oil; you may need to get eye level with skillet to see this. Turn on your stove's vent hood, if you have one.)

8. Use spatula to transfer 6 patties to skillet. Sprinkle patties evenly with ¼ cup chopped onion. Use back of spatula to press onion firmly into patties. Cook patties, without moving them, for 2 minutes.

9. Reduce heat to medium. Use clean spatula to carefully flip patties. Top each patty with 2 slices of cheese and 1 bun top.

10. Carefully pour 2 tablespoons water into empty spot in skillet (do not wet buns) and cover skillet with lid. Cook, covered, until burgers are cooked through and cheese is melted, about 2 minutes. Turn off heat.

11. Use oven mitts to remove lid. Transfer burgers to bun bottoms. Cover burgers with large piece of aluminum foil to keep warm.

12. Use spatula to carefully scrape browned bits out of skillet and discard (skillet will be hot!). Repeat steps 7 through 11 to cook second batch of sliders with remaining 1 teaspoon oil, 6 patties, ¼ cup onion, American cheese, bun tops, and 2 tablespoons water. Serve immediately.

STEAM YOUR SLIDERS

These cheesy, onion-studded sliders are inspired by the ones made famous by White Castle, which has been slinging mini burgers since 1921. To give our sliders their iconic gooey cheese and pillowy buns, we enlisted the power of steam. Adding a splash of water and putting a lid on the skillet traps the hot steam, quickly melting the cheese and gently softening the bun tops. (Just make sure not to splash the bread!) And if you really want to replicate the fast food experience at home, serve these sliders with French Fries (see page 148).

HOW TO SHAPE SLIDERS

Place 1 ball in zipper-lock plastic bag and fold top of bag over ball. Use clear pie plate to press ball into even 4-inch circle, about ¼ inch thick. Remove patty from zipper-lock bag and return to rimmed baking sheet.

PAN-SEARED STRIP STEAKS

BEFORE YOU BEGIN

▶ You can substitute boneless rib-eye steaks of a similar thickness for the strip steaks, if desired.

"Perfectly cooked and well browned—this was an extremely interesting way to cook a steak!"
—Acacia, 15

PREPARE INGREDIENTS

2 (12-ounce) boneless strip steaks, about 1½ inches thick

1 teaspoon pepper

¼ teaspoon kosher salt

HOW TO FLIP STEAKS

Use tongs to flip steaks every 2 minutes until well browned and meat registers 120 to 125 degrees on instant-read thermometer for medium-rare (see page 10).

START COOKING!

1. Place steaks on large plate. Use paper towels to pat both sides of steak dry. Sprinkle steaks evenly with half of pepper. Flip steaks and sprinkle evenly with remaining pepper.

2. Place steaks 1 inch apart in 12-inch nonstick skillet. Wash your hands. Turn heat to high and cook steaks for 2 minutes. Use tongs to flip steaks (see photo, left) and cook on second side for 2 minutes.

3. Reduce heat to medium. Flip steaks and continue to cook, flipping every 2 minutes, until well browned and meat registers 120 to 125 degrees on instant-read thermometer for medium-rare (see page 10), 4 to 10 minutes longer. (Steaks should be sizzling gently in skillet; if not, increase heat slightly. If skillet starts to smoke, turn heat down.)

4. Turn off heat. Transfer steaks to cutting board. Let steaks rest for 5 minutes. Use chef's knife to slice steaks crosswise (the short way) into thin strips (see photo, page 118). Sprinkle sliced steak evenly with salt. Serve.

HOW TO COOK A THICK-CUT STEAK? START COLD. THEN FLIP.

The best steaks are all about the contrast between a crusty, browned exterior and a juicy, pink interior. In this recipe, we use a few outside-the-box tricks to help us achieve our steak goals.

Cold Start: Starting the steaks in a cold skillet allows them to heat up gradually, making them less likely to overcook in the time that it takes to get that beautiful browned exterior.

Frequent Flips: Flipping the steaks every two minutes gives each side a break from the skillet's superhot surface. This slowly builds that flavorful browned crust without overcooking the interior.

Use Nonstick: The slick surface of the nonstick skillet prevents the steaks from sticking (key when you're flipping every two minutes!) and lets you cook without adding splattery, smoky oil. Plus, all of the savory browned bits will stick to the steaks, not the pan.

OVEN-ROASTED SALMON

with Mango-Mint Salsa

BEFORE YOU BEGIN

▶ This recipe was developed using farmed salmon; if you're using leaner wild-caught salmon, cook it until the thickest parts of the fillets register 120 degrees for the best results.

SUPERIOR SALMON

To achieve salmon perfection, we first heat the oven—and the rimmed baking sheet—to a whopping 500 degrees. Then, we drop the temperature to 275 degrees, place the salmon fillets on the hot baking sheet, and let them cook for just about 10 minutes. The intense blast of heat from the hot oven and preheated baking sheet quickly firms up the salmon's exterior. Then, as the oven temperature slowly drops, the inside of the fish gently cooks, leaving you with perfectly cooked salmon waiting for a spoonful of refreshing salsa.

PREPARE INGREDIENTS

1   mango, cut into ¼-inch pieces
    (see photo, below)

3   tablespoons lime juice, squeezed
    from 2 limes

2   tablespoons chopped fresh mint
    (see page 13)

1   jalapeño chile, stemmed, seeded,
    and minced (see page 14)

1   tablespoon plus 2 teaspoons extra-virgin
    olive oil, measured separately

1   garlic clove, peeled and minced
    (see page 13)

½   teaspoon plus ½ teaspoon salt,
    measured separately

4   (6- to 8-ounce) center-cut skin-on
    salmon fillets, 1 to 1½ inches thick

¼   teaspoon pepper

HOW TO PREP A MANGO

Place mango on cutting board. Use chef's knife to slice around pit to remove 2 large pieces. Discard pit. Cut ¼-inch crosshatch pattern into flesh of each each piece (don't cut through skin). Insert spoon between skin and flesh and scoop out mango cubes.

START COOKING!

1. Line rimmed baking sheet with aluminum foil. Adjust oven rack to lowest position, place foil-lined baking sheet on rack, and heat oven to 500 degrees.

2. In medium bowl, use spoon to stir together mango, lime juice, mint, jalapeño, 1 tablespoon oil, garlic, and ½ teaspoon salt.

3. Use paper towels to pat salmon dry. Rub fillets evenly on both sides with remaining 2 teaspoons oil. Sprinkle flesh sides evenly with pepper and remaining ½ teaspoon salt. Wash your hands.

4. When oven reaches 500 degrees, reduce oven temperature to 275 degrees. Working quickly, use oven mitts to pull out oven rack and carefully place salmon fillets, skin side down, onto hot baking sheet. Slide rack back into oven and roast until thickest parts of fillets register 125 degrees on instant-read thermometer (see page 10), 9 to 13 minutes.

5. Transfer baking sheet to cooling rack. Slide spatula underneath each fillet to detach from skin, leaving skin behind on foil, and transfer fillets to serving plates. Top fillets with mango salsa and serve.

"Hearing the salmon sizzle on the hot pan was awesome!"
—Collin, 14

SHRIMP AND GRITS

with Andouille Cream Sauce

BEFORE YOU BEGIN

▶ Make sure to thaw your shrimp before you start this recipe. The best way to thaw shrimp is overnight in the refrigerator.

▶ Here are a few brands of Louisiana seasoning (often labeled Cajun or Creole seasoning): Tony Chachere's Original Creole Seasoning, McCormick Perfect Pinch Cajun Seasoning, or Zataran's Creole Seasoning.

"The rolling texture of the grits combined with the andouille cream sauce created a combination of a sweet and umami."
—Alexander, 15

PREPARE INGREDIENTS

- 1 pound frozen peeled and deveined, extra-large shrimp (21 to 25 per pound), thawed and tails removed
- 1 teaspoon Louisiana seasoning
- 4 cups water
- ½ teaspoon salt
- 1 cup old-fashioned grits
- ¼ teaspoon pepper
- 2 tablespoons plus ¾ cup heavy cream, measured separately
- 1 tablespoon unsalted butter
- 2 ounces andouille sausage, cut into ½-inch pieces (½ cup)
- 1 scallion, root end trimmed, white and green parts separated and sliced thin
- 1 garlic clove, peeled and minced (see page 13)
- ½ teaspoon hot sauce, plus extra for serving

GREAT GRITS

Old-fashioned grits are a dried and ground corn product similar to (but not interchangeable with) cornmeal and polenta. They create this dish's creamy base—if you know how to cook them! Whisking grits often as they cook prevents lumps from forming and stops the grits from sticking to the saucepan. And cooking grits slowly over medium-low heat releases some of their starch, which amps up their creamy texture. A bit of heavy cream makes the grits even more luscious—and that's before they're topped with a smoky, spicy gravy featuring andouille sausage and shrimp!

START COOKING!

1. In medium bowl, use rubber spatula to combine thawed shrimp and Louisiana seasoning. Refrigerate until ready to use.

2. In large saucepan, combine water and salt. Bring to boil over medium-high heat. Slowly pour grits into saucepan, whisking constantly and breaking up any lumps.

3. Reduce heat to medium-low and cook, whisking often and making sure to scrape sides and bottom of saucepan, until grits are tender and thick like pancake batter, 20 to 25 minutes.

4. Turn off heat and slide saucepan to cool burner. Add pepper and 2 tablespoons cream and whisk to combine. Cover saucepan with lid to keep warm.

5. In 10-inch nonstick skillet, melt butter over medium heat. Add sausage and cook, stirring occasionally with clean rubber spatula, until lightly browned, 3 to 5 minutes.

6. Add scallion whites and garlic to skillet and cook until fragrant, about 1 minute. Add shrimp and remaining ¾ cup cream and stir to combine. Cook, stirring occasionally, until shrimp are pink and sauce is slightly thickened, 4 to 6 minutes.

7. Turn off heat and slide skillet to cool burner. Stir in hot sauce and season with salt and pepper to taste (see page 15).

8. If grits have thickened up too much, whisk in up to ¼ cup warm water, 1 tablespoon at a time, until creamy.

9. Divide grits among serving bowls. Spoon shrimp-and-cream sauce over grits, and sprinkle with scallion greens. Serve, passing extra hot sauce separately.

CACIO E PEPE
(Spaghetti with Pecorino Romano and Black Pepper)

BEFORE YOU BEGIN

▶ Make sure to use imported Pecorino Romano cheese, made from sheep's milk—it's saltier, tangier, and more flavorful than domestic Romano cheese made from cow's milk.

"It was a cheesy, peppery experience. Everyone who ate it enjoyed it thoroughly."
—Elias, 14

PREPARE INGREDIENTS

- 2 cups finely grated Pecorino Romano cheese (4 ounces), plus extra for serving
- 8 cups water
- 1 pound spaghetti
- 1½ teaspoons salt
- 2 tablespoons heavy cream
- 2 teaspoons extra-virgin olive oil
- 1½ teaspoons pepper

START COOKING!

1. Add Pecorino to medium bowl. Set colander in large bowl and place in sink.

2. In large pot, bring water to boil over medium-high heat. Add pasta and salt and use tongs to bend pasta until submerged in water. Cook, stirring frequently, until pasta is al dente (tender but still a bit chewy), 10 to 12 minutes. Turn off heat.

3. Use oven mitts to drain pasta in colander set in bowl, reserving pasta cooking water in bowl. Remove colander. Pour 1½ cups cooking water into 2-cup liquid measuring cup and discard remaining water. Add pasta to now-empty bowl.

4. Slowly pour 1 cup reserved pasta cooking water into medium bowl with Pecorino, whisking constantly, until mixture is smooth. Add cream, oil, and pepper and whisk until well combined.

5. Slowly pour sauce over pasta in large bowl, using tongs to constantly toss pasta and sauce. Continue to toss pasta with sauce until creamy, 1 to 2 minutes (see photo, right). If needed, add remaining ½ cup pasta cooking water, a little bit at a time, until sauce is loosened slightly and coats pasta well. Serve, passing extra Pecorino separately.

MASTER A ROMAN CLASSIC

Cacio e pepe is a classic Roman dish that is deceptively simple. Just a handful of ingredients come together to make a dish that tastes sophisticatedly complex.

For an ultrasmooth sauce, we made a few nontraditional tweaks to our recipe. First, we cut the amount of water for boiling the pasta. This ups the amount of starch in the water, which, when added to the Pecorino, helps prevent the cheese from clumping. We also added a bit of heavy cream—it contains molecules called lipoproteins that encourage the proteins and the fat in our sauce to bond together instead of breaking into greasy clumps. Finally, a bit of extra-virgin olive oil, which often has a peppery flavor, highlights the pepe (Italian for "pepper") in this iconic dish.

HOW TO TOSS PASTA

Slowly pour sauce over pasta in large bowl, using tongs to constantly toss pasta and sauce. Continue to toss pasta with sauce until creamy, 1 to 2 minutes.

PASTA *with* SAUSAGE RAGU

BEFORE YOU BEGIN

▶ If you can't find ground Italian sausage, you can use 1 pound of sausage links; use kitchen shears to cut open the casings and peel off and discard casings before adding to the saucepan in step 1.

PREPARE INGREDIENTS

- 1 tablespoon extra-virgin olive oil, plus extra for serving
- 1 pound ground sweet or hot Italian sausage
- 1 small onion, peeled and chopped fine (see page 13)
- 1 teaspoon fennel seeds
- ¼ teaspoon plus 1 tablespoon salt, measured separately
- 1 tablespoon tomato paste
- 2 garlic cloves, peeled and minced (see page 13)
- ¾ teaspoon dried oregano
- 1 (14.5-ounce) can crushed tomatoes
- 1½ cups water, plus 4 quarts water for cooking pasta, measured separately
- 1 pound pappardelle or tagliatelle pasta

  Grated Parmesan cheese

  Chopped fresh basil (see page 13)

QUICK(ER) RAGU

Traditionally, a ragu is a slow-cooked meat sauce—2 to 3 hours of simmering is pretty common—that's served with pasta. Italian American families sometimes call it "Sunday gravy," since a weekend is a good time to make it. For a version that's on your plate faster, we started with ground sausage instead of a larger cut of meat such as pork ribs or beef roast, which take much longer to cook. A quick (at least in the world of ragu) 45-minute simmer transforms the contents of your saucepan into a thick, meaty sauce that tastes like it took all day to make.

START COOKING!

1. In large saucepan, heat oil over medium-high heat until shimmering, about 2 minutes (oil should be hot but not smoking). Add sausage and cook, breaking up sausage with wooden spoon, until meat begins to sizzle and brown, 8 to 12 minutes.

2. Add onion, fennel seeds, and ¼ teaspoon salt and cook, stirring occasionally, until onion is softened, about 5 minutes.

3. Add tomato paste, garlic, and oregano and cook, stirring constantly, until fragrant, about 30 seconds.

4. Stir in crushed tomatoes and 1½ cups water, scraping up browned bits on bottom of saucepan. Bring to simmer (small bubbles should break often across surface of mixture). Reduce heat to low and cook, stirring occasionally, until thickened, about 45 minutes. Turn off heat. Cover with lid to keep warm.

5. Meanwhile (about halfway through simmering the sauce), set colander in sink. Add remaining 4 quarts water to large pot. Bring to boil over high heat.

6. Carefully add pasta and remaining 1 tablespoon salt to pot. Cook, stirring often with tongs, until pasta is al dente (tender but still a bit chewy), 10 to 12 minutes. Turn off heat.

7. Use ladle to carefully transfer 1 cup pasta cooking water to liquid measuring cup. Use oven mitts to drain pasta in colander. Return drained pasta to now-empty pot.

8. Add sauce and ½ cup reserved cooking water to drained pasta. Use tongs to toss until pasta is well coated with sauce. If needed, add remaining ½ cup cooking water, a little bit at a time, until sauce is loosened slightly and coats pasta well. Season with salt and pepper to taste (see page 15). Serve, topping individual portions with Parmesan and basil and drizzling with extra oil.

ADVANCED

VEGETARIAN

BIANG BIANG MIAN

(Flat Hand-Pulled Noodles)

BEFORE YOU BEGIN

▶ Shaping these noodles takes practice. Don't be discouraged if your noodles aren't shaped perfectly, they'll still taste great!

▶ This is a two-day project. Your dough will need to be refrigerated for at least 12 hours (or up to 24 hours) before you can shape your noodles.

PREPARE INGREDIENTS

DOUGH

2⅓ cups (12¾ ounces) bread flour

¾ teaspoon salt

1 cup water

1 tablespoon vegetable oil

CHILI VINAIGRETTE

2 tablespoons chili oil

½ teaspoon cayenne pepper

¼ cup vegetable oil

2 garlic cloves, peeled and chopped coarse (see page 13)

1 (1-inch) piece fresh ginger, peeled and cut into ½-inch pieces (see page 94)

1 tablespoon Sichuan peppercorns (optional)

1 star anise pod

½ cinnamon stick

2 tablespoons soy sauce

2 tablespoons Chinese black vinegar

1 tablespoon toasted sesame oil

1 teaspoon sugar

TO FINISH

Vegetable oil spray

4 quarts water

1 tablespoon salt

12 fresh cilantro sprigs, trimmed and cut into 2-inch pieces

6 scallions, root ends trimmed and scallions sliced thin

START COOKING!

DAY 1

1. For the dough: In bowl of stand mixer, whisk flour and ¾ teaspoon salt together. Add water and oil. Lock bowl into place and attach dough hook to stand mixer.

2. Mix on low speed until no dry flour remains, 1 to 2 minutes. Increase speed to medium and knead dough until smooth, 10 to 12 minutes. Transfer dough to clean counter and use your hands to knead dough for 30 seconds, then form dough into 9-inch log. Wrap dough in plastic wrap and refrigerate for at least 12 hours or up to 24 hours.

3. For the chili vinaigrette: In medium heatproof bowl, add chili oil and cayenne. Set fine-mesh strainer over bowl.

4. In small saucepan, combine vegetable oil, garlic, ginger, Sichuan peppercorns (if using), star anise pod, and cinnamon stick. Heat over medium-high heat until sizzling. Reduce heat to low and cook until garlic is beginning to brown, 10 to 12 minutes. Turn off heat.

5. Carefully pour oil mixture through strainer set over bowl. Discard solids in strainer. Let cool for 10 minutes. Use spoon to stir in soy sauce, vinegar, sesame oil, and sugar until combined. Cover bowl with plastic wrap and refrigerate for up to 24 hours.

keep going >>>

6. To finish: Transfer vinaigrette to large bowl; set aside. Lightly spray counter with vegetable oil spray. Unwrap dough (reserve plastic wrap) and place on lightly oiled counter. Use bench scraper or chef's knife to divide dough into 6 equal pieces (each piece should be 1½ inches wide—use ruler to measure accurately). Spray reserved plastic wrap with vegetable oil spray. Cover dough pieces with greased plastic wrap and let rest for 20 to 30 minutes.

7. Meanwhile, in large pot, bring water and 1 tablespoon salt to boil. Reduce heat to low and cover with lid to keep hot. Pull and cut noodles, following photos, right.

8. Increase heat to high and return water to boil. Add half of noodles to water and cook, stirring occasionally with tongs, until noodles float, about 1 minute.

9. Use tongs to transfer noodles to bowl with chili vinaigrette. Toss until noodles are well coated.

10. Return water to boil and repeat cooking with remaining half of noodles, transferring noodles to large bowl. Turn off heat.

11. Toss until all noodles are well coated with chili vinaigrette. Serve, topping individual portions with cilantro and scallions.

STRETCH YOUR MIND

Biang biang noodles are a popular dish from the Shaanxi province of China. These wide, flat, chewy noodles get their name from the sound they make as they're slapped against the counter to stretch them. Using bread flour, which contains more protein than all-purpose flour, is key for chewy noodles—and stretchy dough. When flour and water mix, the flour's proteins start to link up, forming a network called gluten. The more protein in your flour, the more gluten develops. But in order to make that gluten network stretchy it needs to relax (you're stretchier when you're relaxed, right?). Letting the dough rest for 12 to 24 hours loosens up the gluten network and also allows enzymes to snip some of the bonds between gluten proteins. The result? A stretchier, more relaxed dough that won't tear or snap back when you give it a good stretch—or slap on the counter.

HOW TO PULL AND CUT NOODLES

1. Working with 1 piece of dough at a time, on oiled counter, use your hands to flatten dough into 7-by-3-inch rectangle, with long side parallel to edge of counter (keep remaining pieces covered).

2. Using both hands, gently grasp short ends of dough. Pull and stretch dough out, slapping dough often against counter as you stretch, until noodle is long and thin, about 3 feet long. (If dough is hard to stretch to this length or is snapping back significantly, set aside on counter and let rest, covered, for 10 minutes.)

3. Place noodle on counter. Pinch center of noodle with fingertips and thumbs of both hands, and push thumbs through dough to create hole.

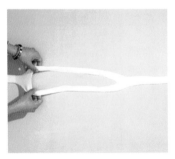

4. Pull apart with even pressure in opposite directions to rip seam in middle of noodle and create one continuous loop.

5. Place noodle loop on counter. Use bench scraper or chef's knife to cut loop in half crosswise (the short way) to create 2 equal-length noodles.

6. Set noodles aside on lightly oiled counter (do not let noodles touch) and cover with long piece of plastic wrap. Repeat stretching and cutting with remaining 5 pieces of dough.

VEGETABLE STIR-FRIED RICE

BEFORE YOU BEGIN

▶ Make the long-grain white rice before you start the recipe (see page 90).

"I liked the depth of flavor, and I like that it was kind of sweet."
—Elly, 15

PREPARE INGREDIENTS

- 2 cups cooked and cooled long-grain white rice (see page 90)

- 2 tablespoons soy sauce

- 1 tablespoon hoisin sauce

- 1 teaspoon unseasoned rice vinegar

- 1 teaspoon grated ginger (see page 94)

- 1 teaspoon plus 2 teaspoons vegetable oil, measured separately

- 2 large eggs, lightly beaten with fork

- 2 carrots, peeled, cut in half lengthwise, and cut into ¼-inch-thick pieces

- 1 cup frozen peas, thawed

- 2 garlic cloves, peeled and minced (see page 13)

- 2 ounces (1 cup) bean sprouts (optional)

- 2 scallions, root ends trimmed and scallions sliced thin

ORDER OF OPERATIONS

To make amazing fried rice, it's all about prepping your ingredients ahead of time and cooking them in just the right order (once you turn on the stove, things move quickly!). First up: Cook your scrambled eggs and set them aside—you don't want them to overcook! Next, sauté longer-cooking vegetables, such as carrots, until they're tender but still a little crisp before adding quick-cooking peas and garlic. After that, it's time to add the rice and sauce to warm them through. Finally, the eggs go back into the skillet along with bean sprouts and scallions. Adding these delicate vegetables last keeps them crisp and fresh-tasting.

START COOKING!

1. In small bowl, use spoon to stir together soy sauce, hoisin, vinegar, and ginger.

2. In 12-inch nonstick skillet, heat 1 teaspoon oil over medium heat until shimmering, about 2 minutes (oil should be hot but not smoking). Swirl skillet to coat bottom evenly with oil.

3. Add lightly beaten eggs to skillet and cook without stirring until eggs begin to set, about 20 seconds. Use rubber spatula to scramble eggs and break into small pieces. Cook, stirring constantly, until eggs are cooked through but not browned, about 1 minute. Scrape eggs into second small bowl.

4. Add remaining 2 teaspoons oil to now-empty skillet. Increase heat to medium-high and heat until shimmering, about 1 minute.

5. Add carrots and cook, stirring often, until slightly softened and spotty brown, 2 to 4 minutes. Add peas and garlic and cook, stirring constantly, for 30 seconds.

6. Add rice and soy sauce mixture to skillet, breaking up any large clumps and stirring to coat rice evenly with sauce. Cook, stirring occasionally, until heated through, about 3 minutes. Add eggs, bean sprouts (if using), and scallions and cook, stirring constantly, for 1 minute. Turn off heat. Serve.

> ▶ ▶ ▶ *UP YOUR GAME*
> You can customize your fried rice by adding your favorite vegetables. In place of carrots, try 1 cup of **sliced mushrooms**; **broccoli florets**; **diced bell peppers**; or **snow peas**, cut in half on the diagonal.

CHANA MAKHANI

(Indian Butter Chickpeas)

BEFORE YOU BEGIN

▶ Serve with basmati rice (a type of long-grain white rice; see page 90) and/or warm naan.

"The texture of the chickpeas in the sauce-like mixture makes for a stunning overall dish."
—Carolyn, 15

PREPARE INGREDIENTS

2 tablespoons plus 2 tablespoons unsalted butter, measured separately and chilled

1 onion, peeled and chopped fine (see page 13)

5 garlic cloves, peeled and minced (see page 13)

4 teaspoons grated ginger (see page 94)

1 serrano chile, stemmed, seeded, and minced (see page 14)

1 tablespoon garam masala

1 teaspoon ground coriander

½ teaspoon ground cumin

½ teaspoon pepper

1½ cups water

½ cup tomato paste

1 tablespoon sugar

1 teaspoon salt

1 cup heavy cream

2 (15-ounce) cans chickpeas, drained and rinsed

2 tablespoons plus 1 tablespoon chopped fresh cilantro, measured separately (see page 13)

IT'S ALL ABOUT THE SAUCE
"Makhani" means "butter" in the Punjabi language, and it refers to this dish's luxurious sauce. Even though butter is in the name, heavy cream is what gives this sauce much of its silky texture. Plus, proteins in the cream keep the sauce smooth, preventing its fat (from the cream and butter) from separating from its water. And blending the sauce guarantees that it's extra-smooth.

START COOKING!

1. In large saucepan, melt 2 tablespoons butter over medium heat. Add onion, garlic, ginger, and serrano and cook, stirring and scraping bottom of saucepan frequently with wooden spoon, until mixture is softened and onion begins to brown, 5 to 7 minutes.

2. Add garam masala, coriander, cumin, and pepper and cook, stirring often, until fragrant, about 1 minute.

3. Add water, tomato paste, sugar, and salt and scrape up browned bits on bottom of saucepan. Whisk until no lumps of tomato paste remain. Bring to boil. Turn off heat and slide saucepan to cool burner.

4. Stir in cream and let cool slightly. Tip saucepan to one side and use immersion blender to carefully process sauce until smooth, 30 to 60 seconds, making sure to keep head of blender and blade completely submerged. (If you don't have an immersion blender, carefully transfer sauce to blender jar. Then, hold lid firmly in place with folded dish towel and process until smooth. Return sauce to saucepan.)

5. Add chickpeas to saucepan and bring to simmer over medium heat (small bubbles should break often across surface of mixture). Cover saucepan with lid; reduce heat to low; and cook, stirring and scraping bottom of pan occasionally, for 15 minutes.

6. Turn off heat. Use oven mitts to remove lid. Add 2 tablespoons cilantro and remaining 2 tablespoons chilled butter. Stir until well combined and butter is melted. Serve, sprinkling individual portions with remaining 1 tablespoon cilantro.

chapter 5

SIDES

HUNG KAO MUN GATI

(Thai Coconut Rice)

BEFORE YOU BEGIN

▶ Do not use low-fat coconut milk in this recipe. Many brands of coconut milk separate during storage; be sure to stir yours until it's smooth before measuring it.

▶ We like the slightly sticky texture of jasmine rice here, but you can substitute long-grain white rice.

PREPARE INGREDIENTS

1½ cups jasmine rice

1½ cups water

1 cup canned coconut milk

1 tablespoon sugar

¾ teaspoon salt

Toppings (see Up Your Game, below right)

START COOKING!

1. Set fine-mesh strainer over large bowl and set in sink. Place rice in strainer and rinse under cold running water, emptying bowl a few times as it fills, until water in bowl is clear, 1½ to 2 minutes. Shake strainer to drain rice well, then transfer rice to large saucepan. Discard water in bowl.

2. Add water, coconut milk, sugar, and salt to saucepan with rice and use wooden spoon to stir to combine. Bring to boil over high heat. Reduce heat to low. Cover saucepan with lid and cook until all liquid is absorbed, 18 to 20 minutes.

3. Turn off heat and slide saucepan to cool burner. Let sit, covered, for 10 minutes.

4. Gently stir rice to incorporate any coconut oil that has risen to top. Serve with your favorite toppings.

JUST-RIGHT COCONUT RICE

Rich, creamy coconut milk transforms ordinary steamed rice into something special: hung kao mun gati. But you can have too much of a good thing—coconut milk is about 25 percent fat, so if you cook your rice in ALL coconut milk, it will turn out oily and heavy. Since our recipe calls for just 1 cup of coconut milk (the rest of the cooking liquid is water), the rice has just the right amount of creamy, coconutty flavor and texture, without being greasy. One quick tip: The fat in the coconut milk can rise to the top of the saucepan during cooking, so be sure to stir it back in before serving.

▶ ▶ ▶ **UP YOUR GAME**

Top your rice with **chopped toasted peanuts, toasted sesame seeds, fried shallots,** and/or **pickled chiles**.

"It tastes great with the toppings suggested. It also makes a batch big enough for my whole family. We're planning to make this recipe over and over."
—Declan, 15

EASY BAKED POLENTA

BEFORE YOU BEGIN

▶ Polenta is a type of coarse-ground Italian cornmeal. You can use coarse- or medium-ground yellow cornmeal or grits in place of the polenta. However, don't use instant polenta or the precooked polenta that comes in a tube for this recipe.

"I liked not having to stir constantly like when it's on the stove."
—Riley, 17

PREPARE INGREDIENTS

4   cups water

1   cup coarse-ground polenta

1   teaspoon salt

    Pinch pepper

1   cup grated Parmesan cheese (2 ounces)

2   tablespoons unsalted butter, cut into
    ½-inch pieces

START COOKING!

1. Adjust oven rack to middle position and heat oven to 375 degrees. In 8-inch square baking dish, use rubber spatula to stir together water, polenta, salt, and pepper.

2. Bake until water is absorbed and polenta has thickened, 30 to 35 minutes.

3. Use oven mitts to transfer baking dish to cooling rack. Sprinkle with Parmesan and butter and whisk until butter is melted and polenta is smooth and creamy. Serve.

NO STIRRING, NO PROBLEM

Polenta is a corn-based dish that originally hails from northern Italy. At its most basic, it's cornmeal and water simmered together until creamy and often finished with butter and Parmesan. To keep the polenta from scorching or turning out lumpy, lots of recipes call for nonstop stirring as the polenta simmers on the stovetop—but not this one! Our oven method is completely hands-off and delivers polenta that's just as smooth and creamy as the labor-intensive stovetop version. How? The oven's heat gently and evenly cooks the polenta from all sides, so there's no scorching and no lumps in sight.

FRIED POLENTA

When cooked polenta is chilled, it becomes firm and sliceable. If you have leftover polenta (or would like to try this with a whole batch), you can chill it in the refrigerator overnight and then cut and fry it for a crispy-on-the-outside, creamy-on-the-inside snack or side.

    Leftover polenta, chilled

1   tablespoon extra-virgin olive oil

1. Place chilled polenta on cutting board. Use chef's knife to cut polenta into squares or rectangles, about 1 inch thick.

2. In 12-inch nonstick skillet, heat oil over medium heat until shimmering, about 2 minutes (oil should be hot but not smoking). Add polenta and cook, without moving, until golden brown on first side, 8 to 10 minutes. Use spatula to flip polenta. Cook until golden brown on second side, 8 to 10 minutes. Turn off heat. Serve.

FRENCH FRIES

BEFORE YOU BEGIN

▶ You will need a large Dutch oven that holds 6 quarts or more for this recipe.

▶ This recipe will not work with sweet potatoes or russet potatoes.

▶ For more information on how to fry safely and how to handle frying oil, see page 11.

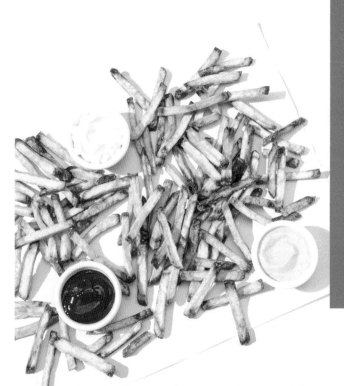

FASTER FRIES

French fries are usually made by dropping cut-up potatoes into a large vat of superhot oil and frying them twice. But restaurant-worthy fries can be yours with just a single fry that starts in a smaller amount of room-temperature oil. As the oil heats up, the potatoes slowly cook through, giving your fries a tender, fluffy interior. Once the oil reaches a boil, the fries' exteriors crisp up and turn golden brown. And with this gentler cooking method, the fries lose less surface moisture, meaning they absorb even less oil than their twice-fried cousins.

PREPARE INGREDIENTS

2½ pounds medium Yukon Gold potatoes

6–7 cups peanut or vegetable oil for frying

Kosher salt

START COOKING!

1. Working with 1 potato at a time, place potatoes on cutting board and use chef's knife to cut into sticks following photos, right.

2. Place cooling rack in rimmed baking sheet and line with triple layer of paper towels. Place on counter next to stovetop.

3. Add oil to large Dutch oven until it measures 1 inch deep. Add potatoes and use tongs to spread into even layer. Cook over medium-high heat until oil reaches a rolling boil (large bubbles should break rapidly across surface of oil). Continue to cook for 10 minutes (do NOT stir during this time).

4. Use spider skimmer or slotted spoon to gently stir potatoes, scraping up any that stick to bottom of pot. Continue to cook, stirring occasionally, until fries are golden and crisp, 10 to 15 minutes.

5. Carefully transfer fries to paper towel–lined cooling rack. Turn off heat and cover Dutch oven with lid. Let oil cool completely (see page 11). Season fries with kosher salt to taste (see page 15). Serve immediately.

HOW TO CUT POTATOES FOR FRENCH FRIES

1. Cut ¼-inch-thick slice lengthwise (the long way) from potato to create flat surface. Rotate potato so it rests on trimmed side. Slice ¼-inch strips from 3 remaining sides to square off potato; discard strips.

2. Cut potato lengthwise into ¼-inch-thick planks.

3. Stack 2 or 3 planks and cut lengthwise into ¼-inch-thick sticks. Repeat with remaining planks.

ROASTED BROCCOLI

with Parmesan, Lemon, and Pepper

BEFORE YOU BEGIN

▶ Broccoli crowns are the top parts of the broccoli plant, without much of the thick, fibrous stem.

BEAUTIFULLY BROWNED BROCCOLI

In the world of food, browning equals flavor. Sprinkling just ½ teaspoon of sugar over the broccoli promotes that delicious browning, and it won't make your side dish taste like dessert. Adding the broccoli to an already-hot baking sheet jump-starts the cooking process, while placing the wedges flat side down ensures maximum contact with the superhot surface—and maximum browning, too.

PREPARE INGREDIENTS

½ teaspoon grated lemon zest, zested from ½ lemon

½ teaspoon plus ¼ teaspoon pepper, measured separately

½ cup grated Parmesan cheese (1 ounce)

1½ pounds broccoli crowns (2–3 large crowns)

3 tablespoons extra-virgin olive oil

½ teaspoon sugar

¼ teaspoon salt

HOW TO CUT BROCCOLI CROWNS INTO WEDGES

If broccoli crowns are 3 to 4 inches in diameter, cut into 4 wedges. If broccoli crowns are 5 to 6 inches in diameter, cut into 6 wedges.

Place 1 broccoli crown stem side down on cutting board. Cut in half through center of broccoli. Place each half cut side down. Cut each half on an angle through stem into 2 or 3 equal wedges. Repeat with remaining broccoli crowns.

START COOKING!

1. Adjust oven rack to lowest position, place rimmed baking sheet on rack, and heat oven to 500 degrees.

2. While oven heats, in small bowl, add lemon zest and ½ teaspoon pepper and use fork to mix until evenly combined. Add Parmesan and toss until evenly distributed. Sprinkle one-third of Parmesan mixture onto serving platter. Set aside.

3. Place broccoli on cutting board and use chef's knife to cut each crown into wedges following photos, below left.

4. In large bowl, combine broccoli, oil, sugar, salt, and remaining ¼ teaspoon pepper. Use rubber spatula to toss until broccoli is evenly coated.

5. When oven reaches 500 degrees, use oven mitts to remove baking sheet from oven and place on cooling rack (baking sheet will be HOT!). Working quickly, use tongs to place broccoli flat sides down on baking sheet in even layer.

6. Return baking sheet to oven and roast until flat sides are well browned and broccoli is tender, 10 to 15 minutes.

7. Transfer baking sheet to cooling rack. Transfer broccoli to serving platter, browned sides up, and sprinkle with remaining Parmesan mixture. Serve.

ESQUITES

(Mexican Corn Salad)

BEFORE YOU BEGIN

▶ We strongly prefer using fresh corn in this recipe, but you can use 4 cups (16 ounces) of thawed frozen corn instead.

▶ If you can't find Mexican crema, you can use a combination of 2 tablespoons of sour cream and 1 tablespoon of mayonnaise instead. If doing so, increase the lime juice to 2 tablespoons.

"It is super delicious because it mixes creamy and acidic and spicy flavors. I really like the texture of the corn as well."
—Pallas, 15

PREPARE INGREDIENTS

- 3 tablespoons Mexican crema
- 1 tablespoon lime juice, squeezed from 1 lime, plus extra for seasoning
- 1 serrano chile, stemmed (see page 14) and cut into ⅛-inch-thick rings
- 4 ears corn, husks and silks removed
- 1 tablespoon plus 1 teaspoon vegetable oil, measured separately
- ¼ teaspoon salt
- 1 garlic clove, peeled and minced (see page 13)
- ¼ teaspoon chili powder
- ¾ cup crumbled cotija or feta cheese (3 ounces)
- ½ cup chopped fresh cilantro (see page 13)
- 2 scallions, root ends trimmed and scallions sliced thin

CORN ON THE GO

Many street vendors in Mexico sell elote—grilled corn on the cob that's slathered in tangy crema, coated with salty cotija cheese, sprinkled with chili powder, and finished with a squeeze of lime. Esquites is a salad with the same components—and the kernels cut off of the cob—but none of the mess! It's sometimes also called elote en vaso or "corn in a cup." In this recipe, charring the kernels in a hot skillet mimics the heat of the grill, and finishing the esquites with fresh chile, cilantro, and scallions brings freshness and color to this summery salad.

START COOKING!

1. In medium serving bowl, whisk together crema and lime juice. Add serrano and set aside.

2. Place corn on cutting board. Use chef's knife to cut each ear in half crosswise (the short way). (If corn is difficult to cut, you can use your hands to snap each ear in half instead, though the cut sides won't be as flat.)

3. Stand 1 piece of corn cut side down on cutting board (so it's flat and stable). Slice downward to remove section of kernels from cob. Rotate cob and repeat slicing until all kernels are removed. Discard cob and transfer kernels to medium bowl. Repeat with remaining pieces.

4. In 12-inch nonstick skillet, heat 1 tablespoon oil over high heat until shimmering, about 2 minutes (oil should be hot but not smoking). Add corn and use rubber spatula to spread into even layer. Sprinkle evenly with salt.

5. Cover skillet with lid and cook, without stirring, until corn touching skillet is charred, 3 to 4 minutes. Turn off heat and slide skillet to cool burner. Let sit, covered, until any popping stops, about 30 seconds.

6. Use oven mitts to remove lid. Push corn to edges of skillet, clearing small space in center of pan. Add garlic, chili powder, and remaining 1 teaspoon oil to center of skillet. Return skillet to medium heat and cook, stirring garlic mixture constantly, until fragrant, about 30 seconds. Stir garlic mixture into corn until coated. Turn off heat.

7. Transfer corn mixture to serving bowl with crema mixture. Let cool for 15 minutes.

8. Add cotija, cilantro, and scallions and stir to combine. Season salad with salt and up to 1 tablespoon extra lime juice to taste (see page 15). Serve.

SUMMER TOMATO SALAD
with Pecorino

BEFORE YOU BEGIN

▶ Use a vegetable peeler to gently shave thin strips from the flat side of the Pecorino Romano or Parmesan cheese—make sure to shave away from you.

▶ Use the ripest tomatoes you can find.

SUMMER IN A SALAD
Tomatoes are the star of this summery salad, so make sure to use the freshest, ripest ones you can find. The simple dressing—featuring olive oil, shallot, and just a teaspoon of lemon juice—balances the tomatoes' tart taste, while savory Pecorino Romano and fresh oregano round out the flavors in every bite.

PREPARE INGREDIENTS

- 3 tablespoons extra-virgin olive oil

- 1 small shallot, peeled and minced (see page 13)

- ½ teaspoon grated lemon zest plus 1 teaspoon juice, zested and squeezed from ½ lemon

- ½ teaspoon salt

- ¼ teaspoon pepper

- ⅛ teaspoon red pepper flakes

- 1½ pounds ripe tomatoes, cored (see photos, right) and sliced ¼ inch thick

- 2 tablespoons shaved Pecorino Romano or Parmesan cheese (½ ounce)

- 2 teaspoons chopped fresh oregano (see page 13)

START COOKING!

1. In small bowl, whisk oil, shallot, lemon zest and juice, salt, pepper, and pepper flakes until well combined.

2. Arrange tomato slices on large platter. Use spoon to drizzle dressing over tomato slices. Sprinkle with Pecorino and oregano. Season with salt and pepper to taste (see page 15). Serve.

HOW TO CORE TOMATOES

1. Place 1 tomato on its side on cutting board. While holding tomato steady, use paring knife to gently pierce top of tomato, near core, at 45-degree angle. Insert knife 1 inch deep into tomato and use gentle sawing motion to make circular cut around core.

2. Use your fingers or small spoon to remove core. Discard core and repeat with remaining tomatoes.

CUBAN BLACK BEANS

BEFORE YOU BEGIN

▶ The little bit of sugar balances any bitterness from the green bell pepper and rounds out the beans' flavor.

"It was quick, easy, and simple. The flavors worked together well."
—Austin, 14

PREPARE INGREDIENTS

2 (15-ounce) cans black beans

2 tablespoons extra-virgin olive oil

1 green bell pepper, stemmed, seeded, and chopped

1 small onion, peeled and chopped fine (see page 13)

2 garlic cloves, peeled and minced (see page 13)

1¼ teaspoons sugar

½ teaspoon dried oregano

½ teaspoon ground cumin

¼ teaspoon pepper

Chopped fresh cilantro, for serving (optional) (see page 13)

START COOKING!

1. Set fine-mesh strainer over large bowl. Pour beans into strainer, reserving liquid. Use 1-cup dry measuring cup to measure out 1 cup beans and set aside.

2. In large saucepan, heat oil over medium heat until shimmering, about 2 minutes (oil should be hot but not smoking). Add bell pepper and onion and cook, stirring occasionally with wooden spoon, until softened and beginning to brown, 5 to 7 minutes. Stir in garlic, sugar, oregano, cumin, and pepper and cook until fragrant, about 30 seconds. Turn off heat and slide saucepan to cool burner.

3. Add reserved 1 cup beans and all reserved bean liquid to saucepan. Use potato masher to mash until beans are mostly broken down and mixture looks thick. Stir in remaining whole beans.

4. Cook over medium heat until warmed through, 2 to 3 minutes. Turn off heat. Season with salt and pepper to taste (see page 15). Serve, sprinkling individual portions with cilantro (if using).

CAN-DO BEANS

When you order just about any meal in a Cuban restaurant, chances are it will be served with a side of saucy black beans. When creating our recipe for Cuban Black Beans, we discovered that canned beans were more than just a convenient shortcut—they also come with a secret weapon, the starchy cooking liquid found inside the can (sometimes referred to as aquafaba). The starch in the bean liquid (plus extra starch released from the small portion of mashed beans) creates this dish's thick, creamy texture.

YOGURT FLATBREADS

BEFORE YOU BEGIN

▶ If you don't have a cast-iron skillet, you can use a 10-inch nonstick skillet instead; in step 6, before heating the nonstick skillet, add ½ teaspoon of vegetable oil and use a paper towel to wipe out the skillet, leaving a thin film of oil behind.

PREPARE INGREDIENTS

- 2 cups (10 ounces) all-purpose flour, plus extra for counter
- ¾ teaspoon baking powder
- 1 teaspoon plus ¼ teaspoon kosher salt, measured separately
- 1 cup Greek yogurt
- 3 tablespoons extra-virgin olive oil
- 1–2 tablespoons water
- 1 tablespoon unsalted butter, melted

YOGURT: A TRIPLE THREAT

Greek yogurt does triple duty in this recipe: First, it adds a subtle, tangy taste without overwhelming the flatbreads' flavor. Next, the water in the yogurt reacts with the baking powder to create bubbly carbon dioxide gas, which gives our flatbreads a lighter, airier texture. Finally, most of the dough's water comes from the yogurt (yogurt is mostly water; the rest is protein, fat, minerals, and harmless bacteria), which means it also helps keep our flatbreads nice and moist.

START COOKING!

1. In food processor, combine flour, baking powder, and 1 teaspoon salt. Lock lid into place and process until combined, about 5 seconds. Add yogurt and oil. Process until no visible streaks of oil remain, about 10 seconds.

2. With processor running, slowly pour 1 tablespoon water through feed tube and process until dough forms ball that clears sides of processor bowl, 10 to 20 seconds. (If dough does not form ball, add remaining 1 tablespoon water and process until dough forms ball, about 10 seconds.) Remove lid and carefully remove processor blade.

3. Sprinkle clean counter with extra flour and coat your hands with flour. Transfer dough to floured counter, knead for 30 seconds, then form dough into ball.

4. Use bench scraper or chef's knife to divide dough into 4 equal pieces. Shape 1 piece of dough into ball (see photos 1 and 2, page 47). Repeat with remaining pieces. Cover dough balls loosely with plastic wrap. Let sit for 30 minutes.

keep going >>>

5. Sprinkle clean counter with extra flour. Use your fingertips to gently pat 1 dough ball into 5-inch circle (keep remaining dough balls covered). Use rolling pin to roll dough into 8-inch circle, flouring counter as needed to prevent sticking. Repeat patting and rolling with remaining dough balls.

6. Heat 10-inch cast-iron skillet over medium heat for 3 minutes (skillet should be hot but not smoking).

7. Cook 1 flatbread following photos, right.

8. Repeat pricking with fork and cooking with remaining dough rounds, stacking flatbreads and re-covering with towel as they finish. Turn off heat.

9. Use pastry brush to paint flatbreads lightly with melted butter. Sprinkle with remaining ¼ teaspoon salt. Serve warm.

HOW TO COOK FLATBREADS

1. Gently prick 1 dough round all over with fork. Carefully place in skillet and cook until underside is spotty brown, 1 to 3 minutes.

2. Use spatula to carefully flip dough round and cook until second side is spotty brown, 1 to 3 minutes. Carefully transfer flatbread to plate and cover with clean dish towel to keep warm.

OATMEAL DINNER ROLLS

BEFORE YOU BEGIN

▶ For an accurate measurement of boiling water, bring a kettle of water to a boil and then measure out the amount you need.

▶ Avoid blackstrap molasses in this recipe—it has a very bitter flavor.

PREPARE INGREDIENTS

- ⅔ cup (5⅓ ounces) boiling water
- 2 tablespoons unsalted butter, cut into 4 pieces
- ¾ cup (2¼ ounces) plus 4 teaspoons old-fashioned rolled oats, measured separately
- 1½ cups (8¼ ounces) bread flour, plus extra for counter
- ¾ cup (4⅛ ounces) whole-wheat flour
- ½ cup (4 ounces) cold water
- ¼ cup molasses
- 1½ teaspoons instant or rapid-rise yeast
- 1 teaspoon salt

  Vegetable oil spray

- 1 large egg, cracked into bowl and lightly beaten with fork

NOT YOUR AVERAGE DINNER ROLL

Oatmeal is for more than just breakfast and cookies—it also makes these dinner rolls extra-soft and extra-moist. As the raw oats soak, they absorb the boiling water and puff up, locking in lots of moisture without making the dough too soggy to shape. The plush, pillowy rolls get their slightly nutty flavor from whole-wheat flour, while molasses adds a touch of sweetness. Finally, a sprinkle of oats on top gives them an extra hit of crunchy texture.

START COOKING!

1. In bowl of stand mixer, use rubber spatula to stir together boiling water, butter, and ¾ cup oats. Let sit until butter is melted and most of water has been absorbed, about 10 minutes.

2. Add bread flour, whole-wheat flour, cold water, molasses, yeast, and salt. Lock bowl in place and attach dough hook to stand mixer. Mix on low speed until no dry flour is visible, about 1 minute. Increase speed to medium-low and knead dough for 8 minutes.

3. Spray large bowl with vegetable oil spray. Use rubber spatula to scrape dough into greased bowl. Cover bowl with plastic wrap. Let dough rise on counter until doubled in size, 1 to 1¼ hours.

4. Spray 9-inch round cake pan with vegetable oil spray and set aside. Sprinkle clean counter lightly with extra bread flour. Transfer dough to lightly floured counter (save plastic wrap for step 6). Gently pat dough into even 8-inch square. Use bench scraper or chef's knife to divide dough into 12 equal pieces (3 rows by 4 rows; about 2¼ ounces each, if using kitchen scale).

keep going >>>

5. Working with 1 piece of dough at a time on clean counter, form dough pieces into smooth, tight balls (see photos 1 and 2, page 47).

6. Arrange dough balls, seam sides down, in greased cake pan, placing 9 dough balls around edge of pan and remaining 3 dough balls in center. Cover pan with reserved plastic wrap and let rise until rolls are doubled in size and no gaps are visible between them, 45 minutes to 1¼ hours.

7. While rolls rise, adjust oven rack to lower-middle position and heat oven to 375 degrees. When rolls are ready, remove plastic wrap and use pastry brush to brush tops with beaten egg. Sprinkle evenly with remaining 4 teaspoons oats.

8. Bake until rolls are deep brown and register at least 195 degrees at center of roll on instant-read thermometer (see photo 1, right), 25 to 30 minutes.

9. Use oven mitts to transfer cake pan to cooling rack. Let rolls cool in pan for 3 minutes. Remove rolls from pan, following photos 2 and 3, right. Let rolls cool on cooling rack for at least 20 minutes. Pull apart and serve warm.

HOW TO BAKE AND COOL PULL-APART ROLLS

1. Bake until rolls are deep brown and register at least 195 degrees at center on instant-read thermometer.

2. While wearing oven mitts, turn cake pan upside down to release rolls from pan onto cooling rack.

3. Turn rolls right side up on cooling rack.

chapter 6
SWEETS

BROWNED BUTTER SNICKERDOODLES

BEFORE YOU BEGIN

▶ Use a light-colored skillet when browning the butter in step 3; a dark-colored skillet makes it difficult to see when the butter has reached the correct color.

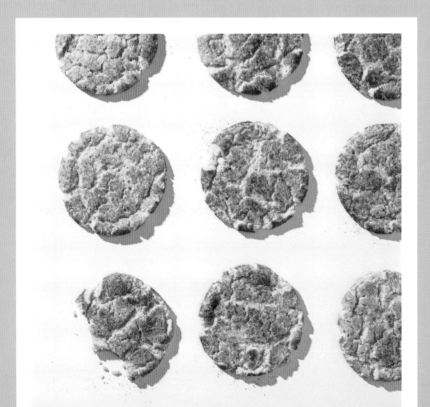

"I liked how the browned butter made the cookies taste, and the cream cheese was an interesting touch."
—Alison, 14

PREPARE INGREDIENTS

1 cup (5 ounces) all-purpose flour

½ teaspoon cream of tartar

½ teaspoon baking soda

¼ teaspoon salt

¼ cup (2 ounces) cream cheese

¾ cup (5¼ ounces) plus 3 tablespoons sugar, measured separately

4 tablespoons unsalted butter, cut into 4 pieces

2 tablespoons vegetable oil

1 large egg yolk (see page 191)

½ teaspoon vanilla extract

1½ teaspoons ground cinnamon

A BUTTERY TWIST ON A CLASSIC COOKIE

Browning butter takes a few more minutes—and a more watchful eye—than just melting it, but the results are worth it. As the butter bubbles in the hot skillet, its amino acids (the building blocks of proteins) react with its sugars to create new, nutty-flavored, brown-colored (and very delicious) compounds that add even more flavor to these classic cookies.

START COOKING!

1. Adjust oven rack to middle position and heat oven to 350 degrees. Line rimmed baking sheet with parchment paper.

2. In medium bowl, whisk together flour, cream of tartar, baking soda, and salt. In large heatproof bowl, combine cream cheese and ¾ cup sugar.

3. In 10-inch skillet, melt butter over medium heat. When butter is melted, reduce heat to medium-low. Cook, stirring constantly and scraping bottom of pan with rubber spatula, until butter solids turn color of milk chocolate, 4 to 8 minutes. Turn off heat.

4. Immediately scrape browned butter into bowl with cream cheese and sugar. Stir and mash until well combined.

5. Add oil, egg yolk, and vanilla to browned butter mixture and whisk until smooth. Add flour mixture and use rubber spatula to stir until no dry flour is visible and soft dough forms.

6. In shallow dish, use spoon to stir together cinnamon and remaining 3 tablespoons sugar. Use your hands to roll dough into 10 balls (about 2 tablespoons each). Drop balls directly into shallow dish with sugar mixture and roll to coat.

7. Place dough balls on parchment-lined baking sheet, leaving about 2 inches between balls. (Arrange dough balls in staggered rows so they do not spread into each other.) Use bottom of drinking glass to gently flatten balls into 2-inch-wide circles, about ½ inch thick.

8. Bake cookies until puffed and covered with small cracks (cookies will look raw between cracks and seem underdone but they will deflate and set as they cool), 11 to 13 minutes, rotating baking sheet halfway through baking (see page 15).

9. Use oven mitts to transfer baking sheet to cooling rack. Let cookies cool completely on baking sheet, about 30 minutes. Serve.

BEGINNER

VEGETARIAN

SKILLET BROWNIE COOKIE

BEFORE YOU BEGIN

▶ If you don't have a cast-iron skillet, you can use a 9-inch cake pan or springform pan. Melt the butter before starting the recipe.

▶ We highly recommend using Dutch-processed cocoa powder in this recipe. If you use natural cocoa powder, the cookie will be lighter in color and drier in texture.

PREPARE INGREDIENTS

- 6 tablespoons unsalted butter, cut into 6 pieces
- 1 cup (5 ounces) all-purpose flour
- 3 tablespoons Dutch-processed cocoa powder
- ¼ teaspoon baking soda
- ¼ teaspoon salt
- ¾ cup packed (5¼ ounces) light brown sugar
- 2 tablespoons vegetable oil
- 1 large egg
- 1 teaspoon vanilla extract
- ½ cup (3 ounces) chocolate chips

ONE SMART (SKILLET) COOKIE

Making one giant cookie might actually be easier than making a whole bunch of regular-size cookies. There's no scooping or rolling dough, and melting the butter right in the skillet has the added benefit of also greasing the pan, preventing our cookie from sticking as it bakes. Cut your Skillet Brownie Cookie into slices and serve with a scoop of ice cream or a dollop of whipped cream.

START COOKING!

1. Adjust oven rack to upper-middle position and heat oven to 375 degrees. In 10-inch cast-iron skillet, melt butter over medium heat. Turn off heat and use rubber spatula to scrape butter into large heatproof bowl. Set skillet aside on cool burner (don't wipe it out or wash it).

2. In medium bowl, whisk together flour, cocoa, baking soda, and salt.

3. Add brown sugar and oil to bowl with butter and whisk until well combined. Add egg and vanilla and whisk until smooth.

4. Add flour mixture to butter mixture and use rubber spatula to stir until just combined and no dry flour is visible. Add chocolate chips and stir until evenly distributed.

5. Scrape cookie dough into now-empty skillet. Spread and push dough into even layer covering bottom of skillet.

6. Transfer skillet to oven and bake until edges of cookie are set and top looks dry and shiny, 16 to 18 minutes.

7. Use oven mitts to transfer skillet to cooling rack. Place oven mitt on skillet handle as a reminder that handle is HOT. Let cookie cool in skillet for 30 minutes.

8. Use butter knife to cut cookie into wedges, being careful not to scratch surface of skillet. Serve.

S'MORES BARS

BEFORE YOU BEGIN

▶ Note that the baked s'mores bars need to cool for at least
4 hours in order to set. If you're in a hurry, you can chill the bars
in the refrigerator for 1 hour, but don't refrigerate them longer
than that because the crust will become too hard.

PREPARE INGREDIENTS

Vegetable oil spray

7   whole graham crackers, broken into pieces

½   cup (2½ ounces) all-purpose flour

¼   cup packed (1¾ ounces) brown sugar

½   teaspoon salt

8   tablespoons unsalted butter, cut into ½-inch pieces and chilled

6   (1.55-ounce) HERSHEY'S Milk Chocolate Candy Bars

1   cup marshmallow crème

1½ cups mini marshmallows

A CAMPFIRE CLASSIC, INDOORS

Nearly 100 years ago, the first recipe for s'mores appeared in the Girl Scout guidebook *Tramping and Trailing with the Girl Scouts* (1927). In this version, we bring the campfire into the kitchen. Instead of roasting marshmallows over an open fire, we spread our bars with fluffy marshmallow crème, top them with mini marshmallows, and let the heat of the oven do the browning work (while simultaneously melting the chocolate).

START COOKING!

1. Adjust oven rack to middle position and heat oven to 425 degrees. Make aluminum foil sling for 8-inch square metal baking pan (see page 174). Spray foil well with vegetable oil spray.

2. Add cracker pieces to food processor and lock lid into place. Process until finely ground, about 30 seconds. Add flour, brown sugar, and salt. Pulse until mixture is combined, about five 1-second pulses.

3. Add butter and pulse until mixture is uniform and resembles wet sand, about twenty 1-second pulses.

4. Remove lid and carefully remove processor blade. Use rubber spatula to transfer cracker mixture to foil-lined pan. Press dough firmly into even layer in bottom of pan.

5. Bake until crust is well browned around edges, 11 to 13 minutes. Use oven mitts to transfer baking pan to cooling rack. Let cool completely, about 45 minutes. (Do not turn off oven.)

keep going >>>

6. When crust is cooled, cover with 5 chocolate bars, breaking bars as necessary to create an even layer (you will have some chocolate left over). Place remaining chocolate (including sixth bar) on cutting board and use chef's knife to chop into small pieces; set aside.

7. Spray rubber spatula with vegetable oil spray. Use greased spatula to spread marshmallow crème over chocolate bars. Sprinkle mini marshmallows evenly over marshmallow crème.

8. Bake bars until marshmallows are puffed and dark brown, about 15 minutes. Use oven mitts to transfer baking pan to cooling rack. Sprinkle with chopped chocolate. Let bars cool until chocolate is set, at least 4 hours.

9. Use foil overhang to lift bars out of pan and transfer to cutting board. Lightly spray chef's knife with vegetable oil spray. Cut bars into squares just before serving. (Uncut bars can be stored in airtight container at room temperature for up to 2 days.)

"Crispy, gooey, and yummy."
—Lexi, 17

HOW TO MAKE A FOIL SLING

1. Fold 2 long sheets of aluminum foil so that each sheet measures 8 inches across and roughly 13 inches long (sheets should match width of baking pan).

2. Lay sheets of foil in pan so that sheets are perpendicular to each other. Let extra foil hang over edges of pan. Push foil into corners and up sides of pan, smoothing foil so it rests against pan.

WHOOPIE PIES

BEFORE YOU BEGIN

▶ We highly recommend using Dutch-processed cocoa powder in this recipe. If you use natural cocoa powder, the cakes will be lighter in color and drier in texture.

▶ If you don't have buttermilk, you can stir together 1 cup milk and 1 tablespoon lemon juice instead.

PREPARE INGREDIENTS

CAKES

2 cups (10 ounces) all-purpose flour

½ cup (1½ ounces) Dutch-processed cocoa powder

¾ teaspoon baking soda

½ teaspoon salt

1 cup packed (7 ounces) light brown sugar

8 tablespoons unsalted butter, cut into 8 pieces and softened

1 large egg

1 teaspoon vanilla extract

1 cup (8 ounces) buttermilk

FILLING

1 cup (4 ounces) confectioners' (powdered) sugar

8 tablespoons unsalted butter, cut into 8 pieces and softened

1 cup marshmallow crème

1 teaspoon vanilla extract

Pinch salt

START COOKING!

1. For the cakes: Adjust oven racks to upper-middle and lower-middle positions and heat oven to 350 degrees. Line 2 rimmed baking sheets with parchment paper.

2. In medium bowl, whisk together flour, cocoa, baking soda, and ½ teaspoon salt.

3. In bowl of stand mixer (or large bowl if using handheld mixer), combine brown sugar and 8 tablespoons softened butter. If using stand mixer, lock bowl into place and attach paddle to stand mixer. Beat on medium speed until mixture is pale and fluffy, about 3 minutes.

4. Use rubber spatula to scrape down sides of bowl. Add egg and 1 teaspoon vanilla. Beat on medium speed until combined, about 30 seconds.

5. Carefully add half of flour mixture to bowl. Mix on low speed until combined, about 30 seconds. With mixer running, slowly pour in buttermilk and mix until combined, about 30 seconds.

6. Scrape down sides of bowl. Add remaining half of flour mixture. Mix on low speed until combined and no dry flour is visible, about 30 seconds. Remove bowl from stand mixer (if using). Scrape down sides of bowl and stir in any remaining dry flour.

7. Fill pastry bag or large zipper-lock bag with half of batter following photos, page 178.

8. Pipe 12 equal-size mounds of batter on 1 parchment-lined baking sheet following photo 1, page 179. Refill pastry bag with remaining batter and repeat piping 12 more mounds on second parchment-lined baking sheet.

keep going >>>

9. Bake until toothpick inserted in center of 1 cake comes out clean, 10 to 12 minutes, switching and rotating baking sheets halfway through baking (see page 15).

10. Use oven mitts to transfer baking sheets to 2 cooling racks. Let cakes cool completely on baking sheets, about 30 minutes.

11. For the filling: While cakes are cooling, in clean, dry bowl of stand mixer (or clean large bowl if using handheld mixer) combine confectioners' sugar and 8 tablespoons softened butter. Lock bowl into place and attach paddle to stand mixer (if using). Beat on low speed until mixture is just combined, about 1 minute.

12. Use clean rubber spatula to scrape down sides of bowl. Beat on medium speed until mixture is fluffy, about 3 minutes.

13. Add marshmallow crème, 1 teaspoon vanilla, and pinch salt. Beat on medium speed until combined, about 2 minutes. Remove bowl from stand mixer (if using).

14. Fill second pastry bag or large zipper-lock bag with marshmallow filling following photos, right.

15. When cakes are cool, flip 12 cakes over on 1 baking sheet. Pipe filling onto each upside-down cake, dividing filling evenly between cakes following photo 2, far right.

16. Place remaining 12 cakes on top of filling to create 12 whoopie pies. Press gently to spread filling to edges of cakes. Serve. (Assembled whoopie pies can be refrigerated for up to 3 days.)

HOW TO FILL A PASTRY BAG

1. Use scissors to cut off bottom corner of pastry bag or large zipper-lock bag. Fold top of pastry bag out and halfway down.

2. Stand bag upright in drinking glass (with cut corner touching bottom of glass). Use rubber spatula to transfer half of batter to bag.

3. Twist top of bag tightly to push batter toward cut corner.

FOR PERFECTLY SHAPED CAKES, PIPE

It's easier than it seems to create perfectly round, uniform-size cakes for our whoopie pies. Enter: the piping bag (or a trusty zipper-lock bag). Piping the batter lets you control how much you use for each cake, and also gives you control over the shape—it's much easier to squeeze out a circle of batter than to scoop and drop it onto the baking sheet. And don't worry about the batter's spiral shapes; they will expand and spread into smooth circles in the oven. (Bonus: Piping the creamy filling onto the baked cakes keeps the finished whoopie pies looking neat and tidy.)

HOW TO PIPE AND FILL WHOOPIE PIES

1. To pipe cakes: Hold pastry bag filled with half of batter perpendicular to baking sheet. Slowly squeeze to pipe batter into 2-inch circle. Continue piping into spiral, about 1½ inches tall. Stop piping and pull bag straight up and away from baking sheet. Repeat to make 12 equal-size mounds, spaced about 1½ inches apart, using all batter in bag.

2. To pipe filling: Pipe filling onto each upside-down cake, dividing filling evenly between cakes.

SALTED BUTTERSCOTCH CUPCAKES

BEFORE YOU BEGIN

▶ Extra butterscotch sauce can be refrigerated in an airtight container for up to 1 week. Reheat sauce in the microwave at 50 percent power for 30 seconds to 1½ minutes, stirring every 30 seconds.

"I shared some cupcakes with my friends and they absolutely loved them, as did I!"
—Roan, 15

PREPARE INGREDIENTS

BUTTERSCOTCH SAUCE

1 cup packed (7 ounces) light brown sugar

½ cup (4¼ ounces) heavy cream

4 tablespoons plus 4 tablespoons unsalted butter, cut into eight 1-tablespoon pieces, measured separately

½ teaspoon salt

½ teaspoon vanilla extract

CUPCAKES

1¾ cups (8¾ ounces) all-purpose flour

1 cup (7 ounces) granulated sugar

1½ teaspoons baking powder

¾ teaspoon salt

12 tablespoons (1½ sticks) unsalted butter, cut into twelve 1-tablespoon pieces and softened

3 large eggs

¾ cup (6 ounces) milk

1½ teaspoons vanilla extract

FROSTING

20 tablespoons (2½ sticks) unsalted butter, cut into twenty 1-tablespoon pieces and softened

2 tablespoons heavy cream

2 teaspoons vanilla extract

⅛ teaspoon salt

2½ cups (10 ounces) confectioners' (powdered) sugar

Flake sea salt, for sprinkling

START COOKING!

1. For the butterscotch sauce: In medium saucepan, combine brown sugar, ½ cup cream, 4 tablespoons butter, and ½ teaspoon salt. Cook over medium heat, stirring often with rubber spatula, until butter is melted and large foamy bubbles burst across surface of sauce, 3 to 5 minutes. Turn off heat and slide saucepan to cool burner.

2. Add ½ teaspoon vanilla and remaining 4 tablespoons butter to sauce. Stir until butter is melted and mixture is fully combined, about 1 minute. Scrape sauce into medium bowl, and let cool completely, about 1 hour.

3. For the cupcakes: Meanwhile, adjust oven rack to middle position and heat oven to 350 degrees. Line 12-cup muffin tin with 12 paper liners.

4. In bowl of stand mixer (or large bowl if using handheld mixer), whisk together flour, granulated sugar, baking powder, and ¾ teaspoon salt. Lock bowl into place and attach paddle to stand mixer (if using). Start mixer on low speed and add 12 tablespoons softened butter, 1 piece at a time, and beat until mixture looks like coarse sand, about 1 minute.

5. Add eggs, 1 at a time, and beat until combined. Add milk and 1½ teaspoons vanilla; increase speed to medium; and beat until light and fluffy and no lumps remain, about 2 minutes. Remove bowl from stand mixer (if using). Use clean rubber spatula to scrape down sides of bowl, and stir in any remaining dry flour.

keep going >>>

6. Use rubber spatula and ⅓-cup dry measuring cup to divide batter evenly among muffin tin cups.

7. Bake cupcakes until toothpick inserted in center of 1 cupcake comes out clean, 22 to 24 minutes.

8. Use oven mitts to transfer muffin tin to cooling rack. Let cupcakes cool in muffin tin for 10 minutes. Remove cupcakes from muffin tin; transfer directly to cooling rack; and let cool completely, about 1 hour.

9. For the frosting: Meanwhile, use liquid measuring cup to measure out ¼ cup cooled butterscotch sauce. In clean bowl of stand mixer (or clean large bowl if using handheld mixer), combine 20 tablespoons softened butter, 2 tablespoons cream, 2 teaspoons vanilla, and ⅛ teaspoon salt. Lock bowl into place and attach clean paddle to stand mixer (if using). Beat on medium-high speed until smooth, about 1 minute.

10. Use clean rubber spatula to scrape down sides of bowl. With mixer running on low speed, slowly add confectioners' sugar, a little bit at a time, and beat until smooth, about 4 minutes. Increase speed to medium-high and beat until frosting is light and fluffy, about 5 minutes.

11. Add reserved ¼ cup butterscotch sauce to bowl. Beat on medium-high speed until fully incorporated, about 2 minutes. Remove bowl from stand mixer (if using).

12. Fill cooled cupcakes with butterscotch sauce and frost cupcakes following photos, right. Sprinkle with flake sea salt. Serve.

A FILLING THAT'S JUST RIGHT

A sweet-salty butterscotch sauce takes these cupcakes from plain to next-level—as long as it's just the right amount of gooey. If it's too thick, the filling will be chewy and tough, and if it's too thin, the filling will soak right into the cupcake. To create the ideal texture in our salted butterscotch, we first add just enough heavy cream to dissolve all of the sugar, but not so much that our sauce winds up watery. As the melted butter in the sauce cools to room temperature, it goes from a liquid to a solid, helping our sauce set into a perfectly-textured filling, ready to be scooped into each cupcake.

HOW TO FILL AND FROST CUPCAKES

1. Use paring knife to cut out cone-shaped wedge from top of each cupcake, about 1 inch from cupcake edge and 1 inch deep into center of cupcake. Discard cones (or snack on them!).

2. Use 1-teaspoon measuring spoon to fill each cupcake with 2 teaspoons butterscotch sauce.

3. Use small icing spatula or spoon to spread 2 to 3 tablespoons frosting over each cupcake.

4. Use spoon to drizzle frosted cupcakes with extra butterscotch sauce.

PEAR CRISP

BEFORE YOU BEGIN

▶ We prefer Bartlett pears in this recipe, but you can also use Bosc pears. To tell if pears are ripe but firm, gently press the flesh at the base of the stem with a finger; it should give slightly. Bartlett pears will turn from green to greenish-yellow when ripe.

▶ Serve with ice cream or whipped cream, if desired.

"This pear crisp will definitely be a crowd pleaser!"
—Calista, 16

PREPARE INGREDIENTS

¾ cup chopped pecans, walnuts, or almonds

¼ cup (1¼ ounces) all-purpose flour

¼ cup (¾ ounce) old-fashioned rolled oats

¼ cup packed (1¾ ounces) light brown sugar

½ teaspoon ground ginger

¼ teaspoon ground cinnamon

⅛ teaspoon ground nutmeg

⅛ teaspoon salt

2 tablespoons plus 2 tablespoons granulated sugar, measured separately

5 tablespoons unsalted butter, melted and cooled

2 teaspoons cornstarch

2 teaspoons lemon juice, squeezed from ½ lemon

3 pounds ripe but firm pears (6 to 7 medium), peeled, cored (see photo, right), and cut into 1½-inch pieces

START COOKING!

1. Adjust oven rack to lower-middle position and heat oven to 400 degrees. In medium bowl, use rubber spatula to stir together pecans, flour, oats, brown sugar, ginger, cinnamon, nutmeg, salt, and 2 tablespoons granulated sugar. Drizzle melted butter over pecan mixture and toss with fork or your fingers until mixture comes together.

2. In large bowl, use rubber spatula to stir together cornstarch, lemon juice, and remaining 2 tablespoons granulated sugar.

3. Add pears to cornstarch mixture and toss gently to combine. Scrape mixture into 8-inch square baking dish.

4. Crumble pecan topping into pea-size clumps and sprinkle evenly over pear mixture.

5. Bake until filling is bubbling around edges and topping is golden brown, 25 to 30 minutes. Use oven mitts to transfer baking dish to cooling rack. Let cool for at least 15 minutes. Serve warm.

A PERFECT PEAR

There are dozens of pear varieties, but the ones you'll typically see at the supermarket are Anjou, Asian, Bartlett, and Bosc pears. All four are known for their sweet, floral flavor, but some are better choices for cooked applications (such as this Pear Crisp!) than others. Ripe Anjou pears are extremely juicy, which can lead to a soggy crisp. Asian pears are very firm and crunchy, even after they're cooked. Bartlett and Bosc pears strike the perfect balance: They're soft but not mushy when they're cooked, making them the best choice for this crisp and other baked desserts.

HOW TO CORE PEARS

Place pear on cutting board. Use chef's knife to cut in half lengthwise. Place flat sides down. Cut each piece in half lengthwise. Turn each quarter so core is visible. Slice at angle to remove core and stem.

STRAWBERRY GALETTE

BEFORE YOU BEGIN

▶ Do not combine the drained strawberries with the jam mixture until you're ready to shape the galette.

▶ Juice from the strawberries may leak out while the galette bakes—that's OK! The parchment paper will catch any drips.

"It was absolutely delicious and it wasn't that difficult to make. I had a lot of fun assembling it."
—Katherine, 15

PREPARE INGREDIENTS

DOUGH

1½ cups (7½ ounces) all-purpose flour, plus extra for counter

1 tablespoon sugar

½ teaspoon salt

12 tablespoons unsalted butter, cut into 12 pieces and chilled

6 tablespoons (3 ounces) ice water (see page 12)

FILLING

1¼ pounds strawberries, hulled (green tops removed), halved if small and quartered if large (about 4 cups)

3 tablespoons plus 1 tablespoon sugar, measured separately

⅓ cup strawberry jam

1½ tablespoons cornstarch

¼ teaspoon salt

Ice cream or whipped cream, for serving (optional)

START COOKING!

1. For the dough: Add flour, 1 tablespoon sugar, and ½ teaspoon salt to food processor and lock lid into place. Process mixture until combined, about 3 seconds. Sprinkle chilled butter pieces over flour mixture. Pulse until mixture looks like coarse crumbs, about eight 1-second pulses.

2. Add ice water. Process until little balls of butter form and almost no dry flour remains, about 10 seconds. Remove lid and carefully remove processor blade.

3. Lay long piece of plastic wrap on counter. Use rubber spatula to transfer dough to center of plastic. Gather edges of plastic together to form bundle of dough. Keeping dough crumbs inside plastic, press dough crumbs together to form ball. Flatten plastic-covered ball into 6-inch circle, smoothing out any cracked edges. Refrigerate dough for at least 2 hours and up to 2 days.

4. For the filling: One hour before baking, in medium bowl, combine strawberries and 3 tablespoons sugar. Use clean rubber spatula to toss until combined. Set aside for 1 hour.

5. Meanwhile, adjust oven rack to lower-middle position and heat oven to 375 degrees. Line rimmed baking sheet with parchment paper.

keep going >>>

JUICY SCIENCE

Juicy strawberries are the stars of this galette (a free-form, single-crust pie), but they can make for a soggy, leaky dessert—unless you use the techniques in this recipe.

Macerate: Tossing the strawberries with sugar (a technique called maceration) triggers a process called osmosis, in which the sugar draws out some of the liquid from inside the berries' cells. We reserve a tablespoon of it for brushing the dough, but the rest goes down the drain—instead of into your galette.

Add Cornstarch and Jam: As the galette bakes, the cornstarch, along with the sugar and pectin in the jam, traps some of the strawberries' leftover liquid, leaving you with a set, sliceable galette (once it's cooled).

6. When strawberries are ready, use 1-tablespoon measuring spoon to measure 1 tablespoon strawberry juice into small bowl and set aside. Set colander in sink, transfer strawberries to colander, and let drain while rolling out dough.

7. Sprinkle clean counter lightly with extra flour. Unwrap dough, place on floured counter, and sprinkle with a little extra flour. Use rolling pin to roll out dough into 12-inch circle, rotating dough and reflouring counter in between rolls. Use your hands to gently transfer dough to parchment-lined baking sheet.

8. In large bowl, combine strawberry jam, cornstarch, and ¼ teaspoon salt. Use rubber spatula to stir until well combined. Add drained strawberries and stir gently to coat.

9. Fill and shape galette following photos, right.

10. Use pastry brush to brush dough with reserved strawberry juice. Sprinkle dough and filling evenly with remaining 1 tablespoon sugar.

11. Bake until crust is deep golden brown and fruit is bubbling, about 1 hour.

12. Use oven mitts to transfer baking sheet to cooling rack. Let galette cool on baking sheet for 30 minutes.

13. Use large spatula to transfer galette to cutting board. Use chef's knife to slice into wedges. Serve with ice cream or whipped cream (if using).

HOW TO SHAPE A GALETTE

1. Scrape fruit mixture into center of dough. Spread into even layer, leaving 2-inch border.

2. Fold 2-inch border of dough up and over edge of filling (but do not press dough into fruit).

3. Continue folding, overlapping folds of dough every 2 inches, until you get all the way around galette.

FLAN

BEFORE YOU BEGIN

▶ This is a two-day project.

▶ We recommend an 8½-by-4½-inch metal loaf pan for this recipe. If your pan is 9 by 5 inches, begin checking for doneness at 1 hour.

"The instructions are easy to follow. It was very rich and creamy."
—Megan, 15

PREPARE INGREDIENTS

- 2 quarts (64 ounces) plus ¼ cup (2 ounces) water, measured separately
- ⅔ cup (4⅔ ounces) sugar
- 2 tablespoons warm water
- 2 large eggs plus 5 large egg yolks (see photo, below)
- 1 (14-ounce) can sweetened condensed milk
- 1 (12-ounce) can evaporated milk
- ½ cup (4 ounces) whole milk or 2 percent low-fat milk
- 1½ tablespoons vanilla extract
- ½ teaspoon salt

HOW TO SEPARATE EGGS

In some recipes, you will need to separate the egg yolk from the egg white. Cold eggs are much easier to separate.

Crack egg into small bowl. Use your hand to very gently transfer yolk to second small bowl.

START COOKING!

DAY 1

1. Adjust oven rack to middle position and heat oven to 300 degrees. Line bottom of 13-by-9-inch metal baking pan with clean dish towel, folding towel to fit smoothly. In kettle, bring 2 quarts water to boil.

2. In medium heavy-bottomed saucepan, use rubber spatula to stir together sugar and ¼ cup water until sugar is completely moistened. Make caramel and pour into 8½-by-4½-inch metal loaf pan following photos, page 193.

3. In large bowl, whisk eggs and egg yolks until combined. Add sweetened condensed milk, evaporated milk, whole milk, vanilla, and salt and whisk until incorporated.

4. Place fine-mesh strainer over second large bowl. Pour egg mixture through strainer into bowl. Discard solids in strainer. Pour egg mixture into loaf pan with caramel, using rubber spatula to scrape out bowl.

5. Cover loaf pan tightly with aluminum foil and place in dish towel–lined baking pan. Use oven mitts to pull out oven rack. Place baking pan on oven rack. Carefully pour all of boiling water into pan (see photo, page 192). Carefully slide rack back into oven.

6. Bake until center of custard jiggles slightly when shaken and custard registers 180 degrees on instant-read thermometer, 1¼ to 1½ hours.

7. Use oven mitts to carefully transfer baking pan to cooling rack. Remove foil and leave flan in water bath until loaf pan has cooled completely, at least 1½ hours.

8. When flan is cooled, remove loaf pan from water bath, wrap tightly with plastic wrap, and refrigerate for at least 12 hours or up to 4 days.

keep going >>>

DAY 2

9. To unmold, carefully run paring knife around edges of loaf pan to release flan from pan. Invert serving platter with raised rim on top of pan. Holding loaf pan firmly in place, carefully turn pan and platter over. Let sit until flan releases from loaf pan, about 30 seconds. Remove loaf pan.

10. Using rubber spatula, scrape any remaining caramel from pan onto flan. Use chef's knife to slice and serve. (Leftover flan can be covered loosely with plastic wrap and refrigerated for up to 4 days.)

GIVE YOUR DESSERT A BATH

Flan, a popular dessert across Latin America, is a sweet, creamy custard topped with a caramel sauce. To make sure that our version has a smooth texture from top to bottom, we bake it inside a second baking dish full of water. In the oven, the water lowers the temperature surrounding the loaf pan—even if it boils, its temperature (212 degrees) will always be cooler than the oven temperature (300 degrees). This allows the flan to cook gently from all sides, giving it an even, uniform texture.

But using a water bath can be slippery business, as the loaf pan can slide around the water bath. Lining the baking pan with a dish towel before adding the loaf pan and the boiling water not only prevents slipping and sliding but also insulates the bottom of the loaf pan from the hot surface of the baking dish.

HOW TO FILL A WATER BATH

Carefully pour all of boiling water into baking pan around foil-covered loaf pan. Water should come about 2 inches up sides of loaf pan.

HOW TO MAKE CARAMEL FOR FLAN

1. Bring sugar-water mixture to boil over medium heat, DO NOT STIR. Once boiling, continue to cook, WITHOUT STIRRING, until mixture begins to turn golden at edges, 3 to 5 minutes.

2. Use oven mitts to lift pan slightly above burner and gently swirl sugar mixture until sugar begins to darken and is color of peanut butter, 1 to 3 minutes.

3. Turn off heat. Move pan over cool burner and continue to gently swirl pan until sugar is reddish-amber and fragrant, 30 seconds to 1 minute. Place pan on cool burner.

4. Carefully add 2 tablespoons warm water (make sure water is warm, or caramel will seize; mixture will bubble and steam) and continue to gently swirl for 30 seconds. Pour caramel into 8½-inch-by-4½-inch loaf pan; do not scrape out saucepan. Set loaf pan aside.

KHEER

(Rice Pudding)

BEFORE YOU BEGIN

▶ Basmati rice is traditionally used to make kheer and will give the pudding its signature texture. You can substitute other long-grain white rice, but the texture will be looser.

▶ A skin may form on top of the milk as it cooks; this is normal and you can stir it back in.

▶ ▶ ▶ **UP YOUR GAME**

Kheer can be served plain or dressed up with toppings. During Hindu festivals, such as Diwali or Puja, kheer is often topped with a sprinkle of **slivered or sliced almonds**, **chopped pistachios or cashews**, **shredded coconut**, **raisins**, **chopped dates**, or **fresh or dried rose petals** (make sure that they're labeled for cooking if you use dried). A pinch of **saffron** or a dash of **rose water** can also be added as the pudding cooks.

PREPARE INGREDIENTS

6   cups whole milk

⅓   cup sugar

8   green cardamom pods

⅛   teaspoon salt

¼   cup basmati rice

START COOKING!

1. In large pot, combine milk, sugar, cardamom pods, and salt. Heat mixture over medium-high heat until it just comes to boil (milk will foam up—be careful not to let it boil over), stirring with wooden spoon and scraping bottom and edges of pot occasionally to prevent scorching.

2. Reduce heat to medium-low and stir in rice. Simmer (small bubbles should break often across surface of mixture), continuing to stir and scrape bottom and edges of saucepan occasionally (every 10 minutes at first, and more often as mixture thickens), until rice is soft and pudding has thickened to consistency of loose oatmeal, 50 to 55 minutes (see photo, right). Turn off heat and slide pot to cool burner.

3. Let pudding cool for at least 20 minutes. Use wooden spoon to remove cardamom pods and discard. Serve warm. To serve cold, transfer pudding to medium bowl; cover with plastic wrap; and refrigerate until cold, about 2 hours. (Pudding can be refrigerated for up to 2 days.)

HOW TO COOK KHEER

Kheer is a bit looser than American-style rice pudding. Stop cooking when the rice is very soft and broken down and the texture looks like loose oatmeal; it will continue to thicken as it cools.

KHEER'S SECRET INGREDIENT: TIME

Rice pudding is eaten throughout South Asia, and is known as kheer in North India, Pakistan, and Bangladesh. Just a handful of simple ingredients—milk, rice, sugar, and sometimes whole spices—transform into an ultracreamy dessert. The secret is in the slow cooking: Simmering the rice and milk for nearly an hour allows some of the water in the milk to evaporate and breaks down the rice, releasing a portion of its starch into the surrounding liquid and thickening the kheer's consistency.

APPLE-CINNAMON DOUGHNUTS

BEFORE YOU BEGIN

▶ You will need a large Dutch oven that holds 6 quarts or more for this recipe. For more information on how to fry safely and how to handle frying oil, see page 11.

▶ If you don't have buttermilk, you can stir together ¼ cup milk and ¾ teaspoon lemon juice instead.

PREPARE INGREDIENTS

CINNAMON-SUGAR COATING

½ cup (3½ ounces) sugar

⅛ teaspoon ground cinnamon

Pinch salt

DOUGHNUTS

2½ cups (12½ ounces) all-purpose flour, plus extra for counter

1 teaspoon baking powder

½ teaspoon baking soda

¼ teaspoon ground nutmeg

½ teaspoon ground cinnamon

¼ teaspoon salt

½ cup thawed apple juice concentrate

¼ cup (2 ounces) buttermilk

4 tablespoons unsalted butter, melted and cooled

1 large egg

⅓ cup (2⅓ ounces) sugar

8–10 cups peanut or vegetable oil for frying

START COOKING!

1. For the cinnamon-sugar coating: In shallow dish, whisk together ½ cup sugar, ⅛ teaspoon cinnamon, and pinch salt.

2. For the doughnuts: In medium bowl, whisk together flour, baking powder, baking soda, nutmeg, ½ teaspoon cinnamon, and ¼ teaspoon salt.

3. In large bowl, whisk together thawed apple juice concentrate, buttermilk, melted butter, egg, and ⅓ cup sugar. Add half of flour mixture to apple juice mixture and whisk until completely smooth.

4. Add remaining flour mixture. Use rubber spatula to stir and press until dough begins to form and no dry flour remains.

5. Sprinkle clean counter heavily with extra flour and coat your hands with flour. Sprinkle rimmed baking sheet lightly with flour.

6. Shape and cut out doughnuts following photos, page 199.

7. Transfer baking sheet with doughnuts to refrigerator. Place cooling rack inside second rimmed baking sheet and line cooling rack with triple layer of paper towels. Place on counter next to stovetop.

8. Add oil to large Dutch oven until it measures 1½ inches deep. Heat oil over medium-high heat until it registers 350 degrees on instant-read thermometer.

keep going >>>

9. Remove baking sheet from refrigerator. Use spider skimmer or slotted spoon to carefully add 6 doughnut rounds to oil, 1 at a time. Cook, flipping doughnut rounds every 30 seconds, until deep golden brown, 2 to 3 minutes. Transfer doughnuts to paper towel–lined cooling rack. Return oil to 350 degrees and repeat cooking with remaining 6 doughnut rounds.

10. Return oil to 350 degrees. Carefully add doughnut holes to oil. Cook, stirring often, until deep golden brown, about 2 minutes. Transfer doughnut holes to paper towel–lined cooling rack. Turn off heat and cover Dutch oven with lid. Let oil cool completely (see page 11).

11. Working with 1 warm doughnut at a time, place in cinnamon-sugar mixture, turn to coat on all sides, and transfer to serving platter. Repeat with doughnut holes. Serve warm.

DIY DOUGHNUT SHOP
Apple doughnuts are a favorite fall treat, but with this recipe you can have them any time of year. To make our doughnuts extra apple-y, we head to the freezer aisle. Stirring thawed apple juice concentrate into the dough adds lots of apple flavor, but not a lot of liquid, so the dough is easy to stir together and shape. A quick fry in hot oil and our doughnuts are ready for a toss in the cinnamon-sugar coating. Bonus: We hang onto the bits of dough from the center of each cut-out doughnut and turn them into doughnut holes.

"I enjoyed making the recipe because it was challenging and something new for me."
—Moorea, 15

HOW TO SHAPE AND CUT OUT DOUGHNUTS

1. Place dough on floured counter and sprinkle top of dough with flour. Gently shape dough into ball. Press into 11-inch circle, gently pressing together any cracked edges of dough.

2. Dust 3-inch round cutter with extra flour. Cut out 9 doughnut rounds. Use 1-inch round cutter to cut hole in center of each round.

3. Use bench scraper or large spatula to transfer doughnut rounds and holes to floured baking sheet, separating doughnut holes from doughnuts.

4. Gather dough scraps and gently form into ball. Press dough into 7-inch circle. Cut out 3 additional doughnut rounds and holes and transfer to baking sheet. (You should have a total of 12 doughnuts and 12 doughnut holes.)

The recipes in this book were developed using standard U.S. measures. The charts below offer equivalents for U.S. and metric measures. All conversions are approximate and have been rounded up or down to the nearest whole number.

VOLUME CONVERSIONS

U.S.	METRIC
1 teaspoon	5 milliliters
2 teaspoons	10 milliliters
1 tablespoon	15 milliliters
2 tablespoons	30 milliliters
¼ cup	59 milliliters
⅓ cup	79 milliliters
½ cup	118 milliliters
¾ cup	177 milliliters
1 cup	237 milliliters
2 cups (1 pint)	473 milliliters
4 cups (1 quart)	1 liter
4 quarts (1 gallon)	4 liters

WEIGHT CONVERSIONS

U.S.	METRIC
½ ounce	14 grams
¾ ounce	21 grams
1 ounce	28 grams
2 ounces	57 grams
3 ounces	85 grams
4 ounces	113 grams
5 ounces	142 grams
6 ounces	170 grams
8 ounces	227 grams
10 ounces	283 grams
12 ounces	340 grams
16 ounces (1 pound)	454 grams

OVEN TEMPERATURES

FAHRENHEIT	CELSIUS	GAS MARK
225°	105°	¼
250°	120°	½
275°	135°	1
300°	150°	2
325°	165°	3
350°	180°	4
375°	190°	5
400°	200°	6
425°	220°	7
450°	230°	8
475°	245°	9
500°	260°	10

CONVERTING TEMPERATURES FROM AN INSTANT-READ THERMOMETER

We include doneness temperatures in some recipes in this book. We recommend an instant-read thermometer for the job. To convert a temperature from Fahrenheit to Celsius, subtract 32 from the Fahrenheit reading, then divide the result by 1.8.

Example
"Roast chicken until thighs register 175°F"
To Convert
175 – 32 = 143
143 ÷ 1.8 = 79.44°C, rounded down to 79°C

RECIPE STATS

Per Serving		Calories	Fat (g)	Saturated Fat (g)	Sodium (mg)	Carbs (g)	Fiber (g)	Total Sugar (g)	Added Sugar (g)	Protein (g)
CHAPTER 1: BREAKFAST										
Breakfast Sandwiches	Serves 2	570	40	16	960	28	0	1	1	22
Shakshuka (Eggs in Spicy Tomato and Red Pepper Sauce)	Serves 4	270	13	3.5	840	25	1	6	0	11
Sheet-Pan Hash Browns	Serves 4	310	14	2	450	40	0	0	0	5
German Pancake	Serves 4 to 6	340	12	6	290	42	0	12	9	13
Brown Sugar–Banana Topping	Serves 4 to 6	120	3.5	2.5	50	24	2	16	9	1
Buttermilk Waffles with Bacon, Cheddar, and Scallions	Serves 4	670	35	18	1700	62	0	6	0	25
Whole-Wheat Blueberry Muffins with Streusel Topping	Per muffin	360	12	4.5	400	57	5	27	23	8
Hearty Avocado Toast	Serves 2	320	21	3	300	31	7	4	0	5
Congee (Chinese Rice Porridge)	Serves 4	80	0	0	390	18	0	0	0	2
Jammy Eggs	Per egg	70	5	1.5	70	0	0	0	0	6
Acai Smoothie Bowls	Serves 2	240	5	2	180	48	4	34	8	4
Sticky Buns	Per sticky bun	460	19	8	370	66	1	34	32	7
Overnight English Muffins	Per muffin	160	2	1.5	370	29	1	2	1	5
CHAPTER 2: SNACKS										
Party Mix	Serves 8	300	19	7	270	26	2	3	0	7
BBQ Party Mix	Serves 8	250	13	3.5	370	29	2	5	0	7
Soy-Ginger Party Mix	Serves 8	290	19	7	430	25	2	2	0	7
Chocolate-Cherry Energy Bites	Per bite	100	6	1.5	45	11	1	6	4	2
Blistered Shishito Peppers	Serves 6	20	1.5	0	15	2	1	1	0	0
Buffalo Chicken Dip	Serves 8	280	24	11	710	3	0	2	0	14
Pajeon (Korean Scallion Pancake)	Serves 2	380	22	1.5	480	41	1	2	2	5
Onigiri (Japanese Rice Balls) with Tuna-Mayo Filling	Per onigiri	180	2	0	180	33	0	0	0	5
Onigiri (Japanese Rice Balls) with Okaka Filling	Per onigiri	150	0	0	150	33	0	0	0	4
Onigiri (Japanese Rice Balls) with Ume Filling	Per onigiri	150	0	0	360	33	0	0	0	3
Pizza Pockets	Per pocket	420	24	14	710	37	0	2	2	11
Broccoli and Cheddar Pockets	Per pocket	390	22	14	700	36	0	2	2	10
Ham and Cheese Pockets	Per pocket	400	23	14	670	36	0	2	2	11

Per Serving	Calories	Fat (g)	Saturated Fat (g)	Sodium (mg)	Carbs (g)	Fiber (g)	Total Sugar (g)	Added Sugar (g)	Protein (g)
Slice-and-Bake Cheddar Crackers Per 6 crackers	200	13	9	220	14	0	0	0	7
Slice-and-Bake Everything Crackers Per 6 crackers	220	14	9	220	15	0	0	0	7
Slice-and-Bake Cacio e Pepe Crackers Per 6 crackers	200	13	8	330	14	0	0	0	7
CHAPTER 3: LUNCH									
Kale Caesar Salad with Chicken Serves 2	690	49	9	1220	27	5	4	1	36
BLATs (Bacon, Lettuce, Avocado, and Tomato Sandwiches) Serves 2	580	33	6	820	56	8	8	0	13
Pork Meatball Sandwiches with Picked Vegetables and Herbs Serves 4	580	35	10	1090	38	2	7	3	25
Arepas with Domino (Black Bean and Cheese) Filling Per arepa	290	12	3	760	40	0	1	0	9
Arepas with Reina Pepiada (Chicken and Avocado) Filling Per arepa	280	12	1.5	520	31	2	0	0	11
Gòi Cuốn (Vietnamese Summer Rolls) Per roll	230	8	1.5	510	30	1	4	0	9
Naan Flatbread with Spiced-Yogurt Paneer Serves 1 to 2	290	16	7	520	26	0	4	0	13
Crispy Tofu Bowls with Vegetables Serves 2	550	22	2	1340	78	9	4	0	18
Spicy Burrito Bowls Serves 2	760	32	4.5	1470	104	19	8	1	20
Pickled Red Onions Serves 8	5	0	0	150	2	0	1	1	0
Shiitake-Beef Ramen Serves 2	430	18	2.5	1780	40	5	6	0	28
Chicken Tortilla Soup Serves 2	390	13	1.5	1520	30	4	6	0	37
CHAPTER 4: DINNER									
Spice-Rubbed Roast Chicken Serves 4	590	40	9	770	3	1	0	0	52
Spice-Rubbed Roast Chicken with Dill and Garlic Serves 4	590	40	9	720	2	0	0	0	52
Spice-Rubbed Roast Chicken with Coriander and Lemon Serves 4	590	40	9	720	3	1	0	0	52
Arroz con Pollo (Chicken and Rice) Serves 4	560	12	2.5	1830	67	3	4	0	42
Buttermilk Fried Chicken Serves 4	820	45	7	570	48	1	1	0	53
Steak Tacos with Charred Corn Salsa Serves 4	570	22	6	1160	50	2	7	0	42
Cheeseburger Sliders Per slider	310	18	6	560	23	1	5	1	18
Pan-Seared Strip Steaks Serves 4	240	9	3	170	0	0	0	0	39
Oven-Roasted Salmon with Mango-Mint Salsa Serves 4	460	29	6	680	14	2	12	0	36
Shrimp and Grits with Andouille Cream Sauce Serves 4	440	25	15	920	35	1	2	0	20
Cacio e Pepe (Spaghetti with Pecorino Romano and Black Pepper) Serves 4	560	14	7	780	83	4	2	0	23

	Per Serving	Calories	Fat (g)	Saturated Fat (g)	Sodium (mg)	Carbs (g)	Fiber (g)	Total Sugar (g)	Added Sugar (g)	Protein (g)
Pasta with Sausage Ragu	Serves 4 to 6	430	10	3	770	64	4	5	0	23
Biang Biang Mian (Flat Hand-Pulled Noodles)	Serves 4	460	21	2	1050	54	3	2	1	11
Vegetable Stir-Fried Rice	Serves 2	510	21	5	1500	61	6	11	0	18
Chana Makhani (Indian Butter Chickpeas)	Serves 4	490	36	21	1250	35	7	10	3	11
CHAPTER 5: SIDES										
Hung Kao Mun Gati (Thai Coconut Rice)	Serves 4 to 6	240	9	7	300	39	1	2	2	4
Easy Baked Polenta	Serves 4	200	10	6	840	20	2	0	0	8
Fried Polenta	Serves 4	260	17	7	840	20	2	0	0	8
French Fries	Serves 4	400	19	1.5	15	50	0	0	0	7
Roasted Broccoli with Parmesan, Lemon, and Pepper	Serves 4	160	13	2.5	310	8	3	2	0	6
Esquites (Mexican Corn Salad)	Serves 4	250	17	5	470	21	2	6	0	9
Summer Tomato Salad with Pecorino	Serves 4	140	12	2	350	8	2	5	0	3
Cuban Black Beans	Serves 4	260	8	1	790	43	1	4	1	12
Yogurt Flatbreads	Per flatbread	410	20	9	450	44	0	2	0	11
Oatmeal Dinner Rolls	Per roll	140	2.5	1.5	200	26	2	5	5	4
CHAPTER 6: SWEETS										
Browned Butter Snickerdoodles	Per cookie	200	9	4.5	140	27	0	16	16	2
Skillet Brownie Cookie	Serves 12	200	11	5	85	26	0	16	16	2
S'mores Bars	Per bar	200	11	7	105	26	0	20	6	2
Whoopie Pies	Per whoopie pie	370	16	10	220	52	0	34	28	4
Salted Butterscotch Cupcakes	Per cupcake	700	43	27	340	73	0	57	56	5
Pear Crisp	Serves 8	310	15	5	40	46	7	30	13	2
Strawberry Galette	Serves 6 to 8	330	17	11	220	43	1	19	8	3
Flan	Serves 8 to 10	280	10	5	230	40	0	39	14	8
Kheer (Rice Pudding)	Serves 4 to 6	220	8	4.5	150	29	0	23	11	8
Apple-Cinnamon Doughnuts	Per doughnut	290	14	3	160	39	1	19	14	3

Introducing America's Test Kitchen Kids!

This book was created by a group of passionate cooks, writers, editors, scientists, educators, designers, illustrators, and photographers. Our mission is to inspire a new generation of empowered cooks, engaged eaters, and curious experimenters.

MOLLY BIRNBAUM
EDITOR IN CHIEF

I would eat the Steak Tacos with Charred Corn Salsa (page 116) every night of the summer, if I could. And you know what? After I edited the dinner chapter of this book, I pretty much did. It was summer, the corn was awesome, and this is the perfect recipe to share with friends.

SUZANNAH MCFERRAN
EXECUTIVE FOOD EDITOR

I loved testing the Pan-Seared Strip Steaks (page 124) with my (teen!) son at home. He realized how easy it was, perfected the method, and now he is our steak expert!

KRISTIN SARGIANIS
EXECUTIVE EDITOR

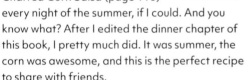

While I loved editing all of the recipes in this book, my favorite is Biang Biang Mian (page 134). They're a project, for sure, but a blast to make—especially with friends. And, even if they don't come out perfectly, they taste fantastic!

AFTON CYRUS
SENIOR EDITOR

I loved working on recipes from a wide range of cultures, including Shakshuka (page 22), Pajeon (page 58), Onigiri (page 60), Cuban Black Beans (page 156), Esquites (page 152), and Kheer (page 194). Cooking food from diverse perspectives is an awesome way to learn about the world and develop your palate!

ANDREA RIVERA WAWRZYN
TEST COOK

As a kid who cooked a lot, I found myself exploring bolder flavors and experimenting more in the kitchen as I entered my teen years. I was thrilled to develop recipes such as Arroz con Pollo (page 108) and Pizza Pockets (page 64), that help teens become more confident and versatile in the kitchen.

CASSANDRA LOFTLIN
TEST COOK

I really enjoyed working on some of the more complex recipes in this book, especially Buttermilk Fried Chicken (page 112) and Shrimp and Grits with Andouille Cream Sauce (page 128). I hope teens will be proud to share them with friends and family.

KRISTEN BANGO
ASSISTANT TEST COOK

My favorite part of working on this book was being a part of the photo shoots for the recipes. Being able to express myself through my jewelry and showing a little bit of my personality added some life to the photos!

KATY O'HARA
ASSOCIATE EDITOR

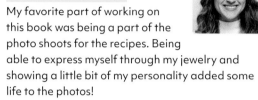

As a breakfast enthusiast, I was thrilled to write some of the content in our first chapter. But it was even better to see the recipes in that chapter come to life on the page. I mean, have you seen those Sticky Buns (page 40)?! (Can confirm, they look just as good when you make them at home.)

TESS BERGER
ASSOCIATE EDITOR

My favorite part of working on this book was learning all about the history of buffalo wings (check out Buffalo Chicken Dip on page 56). Who knew one of my favorite snacks has such a mysterious past?

JACK BISHOP
CHIEF CREATIVE OFFICER

I taught myself to cook as a teenager and I sure wish I had this book. The recipes are approachable but exciting. Younger me wishes I knew about Browned Butter Snickerdoodles (page 168). These cookies are so, so good!

LINDSEY TIMKO CHANDLER
DESIGN DIRECTOR

This book was an absolute joy to work on. We had so much fun exploring the visual direction of the photography—gathering inspiration from pop culture, social media, and the teen forces behind it!

MOLLY GILLESPIE
GRAPHIC DESIGNER, BOOKS

I think this cookbook will remain a trusted and beloved resource, not just for teens while they're teens but also for the adults they're becoming (as a 20-something, I can attest that these recipes are both timeless AND delicious!). It's been such a joy to design this book with them in mind!

JULIE BOZZO COTE
PHOTOGRAPHY DIRECTOR

Teens approach being in the kitchen in a more casual, creative, and independent way than our younger ATK Kids chefs. We really wanted the photos in this book to show how cool and expressive cooking is.

GABI HOMONOFF
ASSOCIATE ART DIRECTOR

My favorite part of working on this book was realizing that I could have been making much better meals for myself after school—if I only had this book!

KEVIN WHITE
PHOTOGRAPHER

Working on the photography for this book was a chance to step away from our traditional look and feel. It was really fun to experiment and collaborate to try new things in the photo studio.

INDEX